Table of C

THE CHARMER
RON MUDDLE

A TRUE LIFE STORY

PETER KEALEY

Foreword

What turns a person from a humble background into a businessman running a multi-million-pound business?

It is an extraordinary person who would put everything on the line to achieve his goals and have the hard-headed business skills, drive and tenacity to gamble his way; who would take calculated risks to make things come to fruition and take decisions that will affect his own future for better or worse. Only a special person with tremendous courage goes down this road and takes these risks. All these traits are part of the businessman's make-up. To set up your own business and expand the business to even greater heights, and then sell the business to make a profit on your investment, is not easy to achieve in these times. This is a true story of such a businessman who put his head on the block to make his business successful, and the ups and downs of his life in his climb up the ladder of success to achieve his goals, from working in his father's garage to owning a business in "the sport of kings".

This businessman is Ron Muddle, who before owning a number of racecourses and introducing the first all-weather racecourse in England was involved in several other businesses in the motor trade, property development and farming. He enjoyed a lifestyle with his family that other people would envy, but it was achieved through hard work. Success can also involve personnel loss, divorce and financial setbacks, all of which are part of this true story and were overcome to lead to greater things.

Ron had become meticulous in his work and was always charming with a smile when involved with business and punctual in his appointments, learning from his father, Albert, to work hard and be on the ball to broker the slightest deal.

The author has used the facts available to give anyone who

thinks it's easy to set up and run your own business a look into the world of a successful businessman and an insight into the ups and downs and the rough and tumble of business. I hope that you enjoy reading the story of Ron Muddle.

1 – Humble Beginnings

Ron Muddle came from a humble family background in the Sussex countryside, where his family had always lived. Ron's grandfather, Thomas, was born in Buxted in 1871 and married Harriet Stevens in 1891. Their first son and Ron's father, Albert Muddle, also known as Bert, was born in Preston near Brighton in Sussex on the 19th of December 1891. Bert then lived in a terraced cottage at 2 Coopers Green in Sussex from 1901.

Thomas was then making a living as a painter and decorator on Lord Portman's estate at Buxted Park. The house came with the job. The "upstairs and downstairs" lifestyle of the inhabitants of Buxted Park was far removed from the life of Thomas and Harriet Muddle. Bert grew up as a country boy with a strict upbringing. Thomas Muddle made friends with Billy Kealey, who worked as a groom at the Buxted estate, and so began a long-term friendship between the two families.

Bert left school at twelve years old and started work plucking chickens for a living before changing jobs. At nineteen he became a farm labourer and he later trained to be a motor mechanic at the Lewes branch of Martin's Garage. He cycled to and from work to his home at Coopers Green. After completing his apprenticeship at Lewes, Bert moved to Martin's Garage, Crowborough, where he learnt to drive a motor vehicle. They hired Bert out as a chauffeur to the Ionides family at Fairwarp, and Bert drove all over England, transporting Nellie Ionides on her holiday outings and other customers requiring a chauffeur service. Bert learnt his mechanical skills in the repair, servicing and overhaul of the motor vehicles at Martin's Garage, which would assist him in his future life.

At twenty-two years of age Bert still was working as a motor mechanic and chauffeur at Martin's Garage when he met and married twenty-five-year-old Leonora Violet Reeve, known to her friends as Vi. Vi had been born at Great Witchingham, Norfolk, on the 22nd of December 1888. She became a seamstress and then left home to go south to Buxted, where she obtained a job as a ladies' maid in a big house. The house was just down the road from Coopers cottages, where Bert and Vi met. They lived with Bert's parents at Coopers Green after getting married, and then moved to 11 Cemetery Lane, Crowborough, where their only child Ron was born on 12th March 1916.

One year later, on the 14th March 1917, Bert joined the Royal Navy as an acting air mechanic at *HMS President 11*. On the 30th of June 1917 Bert was transferred to Vendôme in southern France to a Royal Air Force service base, where he became a first-class air mechanic on the 1st of January 1918. Apart from servicing the planes and preparing them for battle, the air mechanics had to start the engines of each plane by turning the propeller to get the engine on its compression stroke and then spinning the propeller to get the engine to fire up. This was done every time the planes had to be flown into battle, but some pilots, on taxiing down the grass runways, stalled the engines and Bert had to run down the airfield to repeat the starting process again, much to his annoyance.

Bert was discharged from the Royal Navy on the 31st of March 1918 having never fired a shot or seen a German in battle. He returned to Crowborough to work at Martin's Garage as a motor mechanic.

After a year at Martin's Garage, in 1919 Bert started his own garage in converted stables behind The Railway Hotel pub near the railway station at Jarvis Brook. He called it Jarvis Brook Engineering. The company sold and serviced motor vehicles and also owned two cars for taxi work, a Renault and a Ford. The stable stalls were removed from the building to create four car working bays and outside there was enough space to park several cars. To work on the cars Bert jacked up the vehicles and put them on axle stands.

The three terraced cottages at Coopers Green. Thomas Muddle was born in the left hand cottage and then lived in the middle cottage in the early 1900's

Thomas and Harriet Muddle at 3 Coopers cottage Photo taken on the 9th August 1916

The Sopwith Camel F.1 1st World War fighter plane

Bert in his Royal Navy uniform 1914-1918 World War I
A photo of Vi Muddle in her younger years

Then he could remove the wheels to service the brakes and remove the other parts from the vehicles for repair. The only other tools available came from Bert's toolkit.

At this time Bert's family moved to a rented house in Windsor Road, Jarvis Brook. Then, in 1924, Bert built a new garage in Station Road, Jarvis Brook, close to his original premises. He also built a house adjoining the garage called Lyng, which the family moved into when Ron was aged seven.

The garage and house were built by a local builder to Bert's design. There was a central front garage entrance door and another door to the right of the building through which cars could exit the workshop. A one-bay showroom was fitted in the right-hand front of the building and a reception office on the left-hand front side of the entrance door. A pit was fitted in the floor to enable the servicing of vehicles underneath, while other vehicles were serviced and repaired by jacking the vehicles up and putting the cars on axle stands.

Petrol for the cars was delivered to the garage in two-gallon Pratts petrol cans. Later Bert invested in petrol pumps, which required four two-hundred-gallon petrol tanks to be fitted in the ground. Ron remembers that the holes were excavated to fit the tanks in front of the garage, two either side of the entrance door. The tanks were dropped in the holes to await the final installation of the pumps the next morning. But when they awoke the next morning, after heavy rain the following night, they found that the petrol tanks had floated out of their holes and were sitting in the middle of the road. Once the installation of the tanks and the pumps was completed, the fuel was pumped into the fuel tanks by the petrol suppliers, which were Dominion, Shell Mex, British Petroleum and Benzole, so the customer was given a choice of petrol.

Ron's regular job as a youngster was to man the pumps and serve the customers with petrol. This was done by placing the petrol hose in the car petrol tank and hand-cranking the petrol pump until the required amount of petrol had been delivered. Ron had to stand on a box to be able to reach the pump handle. Bert then invested in electric-powered petrol pumps which did not require young Ron to stand on a box to operate the petrol pump.

Ron later had to help Bert repair the vehicles in the garage, and he remembers the repair of a two-speed foot-controlled epicyclic gearbox on a Model T Ford. Ron was responsible for holding a torch over the gearbox in the car while Bert repaired the gearbox and told him to, "Hold the torch steady, son."

Bert's taxis, a Renault and a Ford, were used to ferry local customers to their destinations and they had a contract, amongst others, with the Crowborough Football Club. Ron was still only a kid, but he went to the matches with Bert. One day one of the players did not turn up and Ron took his place. It was the start of his football-playing days and he would go on to play for Crowborough Football Club.

Bert was also an entertainer and he specialised in singing comic songs. He would organise concerts at Jarvis Brook and other venues in the area and get involved in the local carnival, creating his own float. Bert later also achieved the position of president of the local Chamber of Commerce in 1938.

Ron was seven years old in 1924 when Bert started his new business, with Vi's life savings as a deposit and with a mortgage from his building society. It was a big gamble, but Bert succeeded in making a good motor engineering business.

Ron remembers the social get-togethers with his family at his grandmother's. His grandmother would make beef pudding in the copper and sweet apple pudding. Vi used to make the "floaters", which were dumplings that expanded in the stew. At Christmas at Bert and Vi's house a large goose was cooked; the bird was so big Vi asked the bakery next door to cook the goose as she did not have a cooker big enough. The Christmas party at the Muddles' house would finish with a singsong with instruments, with someone

Albert Muddle with Ron aged 3

Bert and Vi Muddle at Jarvis Brook Engineering

Ron on the pumps as a youngster and with Bert as a teenager

playing the piano, Bert singing, Billy Kealey on squeezebox and his son, Jack, on penny whistle. This went on long into the night. They also played cricket matches on the downs with the Kealey and Evans families, at weekends which food and drink was consumed by all.

The family's first caravan made from an
old Morris Cowley truck chassis

Bert made his first family caravan from an old Morris Cowley truck chassis. It had one centre axle, which was used to tow the caravan behind his car, and four corner drop-down supports for when the caravan was parked. At this time in the 1920s the only other caravans (car-a-vans) were gypsy ones drawn by horses. Bert's new concept in caravans that motorists towed behind their cars was years before its time. Albert, Vi and Ron's friends spent many a holiday in their caravan, towing it all around the country to Torquay,

Paignton and far away as Blackpool and to new places every year. Later in his life, Ron built motorised caravans based on Ford 15cwt van bodies in his Kenex factory in Dover, which became a big business in the 1960s until he sold out to his main competitor, Dormobile.

Ron attended junior school from the age of five. He was always bottom of his class, and at the end of his junior school years, after he failed his exams, Vi was called in by the headteacher, Henry Fermor, to discuss Ron's future. Henry Fermor told Vi that Ron was "no academic" but had a "glint of something" which he could not put his finger on, and because of this he would recommend that Ron go to grammar school.

Ron then attended Uckfield Grammar School, but unfortunately Muddle Junior was not one for learning. He was only good at sports and maths, which held him in good stead in his later years, but he did excel at sport. His physical training instructor was a long-jump champion and he created a target for Ron to aim for. Ron went on to become the school long-jump champion, his first big personal achievement.

Ron's first sexual experience was at the age of thirteen when he and a mate arranged to meet two local girls in the forest at eleven a.m. one morning. When they arrive the girls had already removed their pants for the experience, but unfortunately the night before it had rained heavily, making the ground too wet, so sex had to be performed in an upright position, and as hard as they tried, a climax never came, even when they changed partners, so they decided to stop and try another day (which, incidentally, never came to pass).

Ron left school at fifteen and Bert sent young Muddle to the local technical college in Brighton to take an engineering course. Bert then obtained a job for Ron in London at the Shell Mex oil company, which, after a day's work, Ron quit. This did not please Bert and Vi, and it resulted in Ron working in the family business as a motor mechanic.

Ron then met a local girl called Evelyn who befriended

him at fifteen when she was seventeen. Ron's parents approved of her, and every other week, when Bert and Vi went away to Brighton for the weekend, the young couple met at Ron's parent's house and watched television on the settee, enjoying having the house to themselves. Both would remove their clothes and have sex on a regular basis, with Ron taking precautions as he did not want to get Evelyn in the family way. This continued until Ron was seventeen, when Vi bought him his first car. Ron still saw Evelyn, but he would take Evelyn back home early and drive on to Crowborough to meet a girl named Margey. Ron would drive this other girl to a lonely spot where for the next hour or so the two had great sexual encounters in the back of the car.

In 1940, aged twenty-four, Ron obtained a job with the Air Ministry. He would not have obtained the job without his technical college training. He was scared stiff at first of his first job outside the family business, but he soon gained confidence. After six months he was promoted and sent to Bristol on a three-month aircraft training course. After a few weeks he fell out with the RAF instructor, as Ron realised his hands-on experience as a motor mechanic and his technical college training made his knowledge superior to the instructor's.

While working at the Air Ministry Ron was in London on a training course when he accidently met up with Margey, who was training in the voluntary nursing service. They went out to a show and then on to a club and then Margey invited Ron back to her aunt's house where she was staying. Ron had a bedroom next to Margey's, but the next morning when the aunt bought Margey tea in bed she found Ron was sound asleep in Margey's bed. He was forever barred from seeing Margey again. (Margey later married a doctor.)

Ron eventually married Evelyn in 1940 to appease his parents, who wanted Ron to get married and raise a family. Evelyn moved in with Vi while Ron was working in London. But because of Ron working away the marriage did not last and they separated.

Evelyn stayed with Vi until her death in her early twenties from a brain tumour.

On completing his training with the Air Ministry in London, Ron was transferred to a Southampton airport to take up his job as an air crash investigator. There, he cheated death twice.

The first time he was walking the one hundred yards back to his office after talking to the manager and foremen of the factory next to the Vickers Spitfire assembly plant on the airfield when German bombers started dive-bombing the airfield. The manager and foreman were killed, but Ron survived the outside aircraft attack and on entering his office and closing his door a bomb blew out his office wall, going straight out of the opposite window, leaving a hole you could get your head through.

Another near-miss occurred when Ron was on a test flight. The pilot of the plane, who was wearing sunglasses, did not notice the barrage balloons which were installed to stop low flying aircraft such as diver bombers flying over the airfields and flew between the barrage balloon ground-fixing cables, and could have caused the aircraft to crash if the pilot caught the cable with the aircraft's wing but Ron fortunately survived this test flight.

While Ron was working at Southampton, Bert was taken to Pembury Hospital with appendicitis. Ron drove to Pembury to be with his mother and he remembers Bert asking Ron for ten shillings to give to the nurse. On returning to Southampton the same night, Vi phoned Ron to say that Bert had died from a ruptured appendix. It was the 11th of June 1941, and Bert was only forty-nine. Ron returned home to arrange Bert's funeral.

Ron was anxious to move nearer to home to be closer to Vi and he looked to find another position. One day a senior person from the Air Ministry entered the office in Southampton to find Ron on his own with none of the senior managers available. Ron talked to the man, telling him of his family situation and how he would like to move nearer to home. The man said he would see what he could do. The next day Ron had a phone call from the man offering him a position at Gatwick Airport doing the same job, and Ron accepted.

Ron had another near-miss when, on a test flight at Gatwick Airport, the pilot could not get the undercarriage of the plane down to land. Ron was in the rear gun turret with no intercom and could not tell the pilot how to use the emergency landing gear to land the plane or exit the gun turret quick enough. The pilot managed to land the plane on one landing wheel, and then the plane cartwheeled along the runway several times until it came to a stop on its side. Ron exited the plane in one piece, shaken after his third lucky escape.

Vi continued to run Jarvis Brook engineering with her staff until she reached seventy years of age.

The war years broadened Ron's horizons, giving him confidence in himself. He was a man about town and was now looking for the next step up the ladder to take his ambitions further. Ron had become meticulous in his work and was always charming and smiling. He was punctual in his appointments, having learnt from Bert to work hard and be on the ball to broker the slightest deal.

While working at Gatwick Airport, an opportunity fell into Ron's lap which was to change his life. A draughtsman working there designed a reserve fuel tank which could be fitted under the fuselage of a Spitfire to increase its flying distance. The tank could be jettisoned over the sea once the fuel had been used and the pilot could then switch over to the main aircraft fuel tanks to complete his mission before returning to base. The fuel tank was made of wood, as aluminium was in short supply in the war, so if the tank ended up in the sea it would float and could be re-used when recovered.

Ron signed off the Spitfire fuel tank design drawings on behalf of the Air Ministry. An order came back from the Air Ministry for 60,000 fuel tanks. The factory on the airfield only employed a dozen people in production, not enough to produce the volume of tanks required.

Ron asked his line manager who was going to produce the tanks.

The manager replied, "God only knows."

With quick thinking, Ron replied, "If I could get out of this job, would you give me the order to produce these tanks?"

The manager said, "Ron, you know more about the construction than me."

This was the opportunity Ron had been waiting for, and he took the decision to hand in his notice to the Air Ministry.

Ron handed in his one month's notice to the Air Ministry, who said that under Section Y3 he could not leave. So Ron decided to walk out of his job at the end of his notice into his first business deal, despite the fact he had no idea how he was going to set the business up, obtain the contract or produce the fuel tanks. It was a matter of being in the right place at the right time, but also of making a life-changing decision to make the break to become a businessman.

At this time Ron also met Sally, a well-built, strong, attractive lady who came to work in the factory at the airport to manage the first production runs of the Spitfire fuel tank. Sally had a flat in London and invited Ron to meet her at her flat for a night out together. They "wined and dined" and then went to a nightclub before returning to the flat, where a sexual experience occurred which Ron would never forget and which led to an ongoing relationship. The evening was interrupted by a bomb landing outside the flat which frightened the living daylights out of Ron

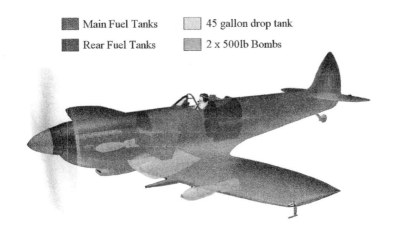

| ■ Main Fuel Tanks | ☐ 45 gallon drop tank |
| ■ Rear Fuel Tanks | ▦ 2 x 500lb Bombs |

The 45 Gallon Spitfire "Drop Fuel Tank" under the fuselage

THAMES
10/12 AND
15 CWT

Carefree

KENEX CARAVAN CONVERSION OF
THAMES 10/12 CWT OR 15 CWT VAN

*Sales Brochure of the Kenex Ford 400E
Carefree Caravan Conversion*

2 – The Spitfire Fuel Tank

Ron returned home and started work in Vi's garage, still thinking about how he was going to manufacture the Spitfire fuel tank. The very same week on the Sunday a customer came into the garage and Ron started talking to him of his idea to produce the Spitfire fuel tank. The customer had evacuated his family to Crowborough but owned a large woodworking company in Folkestone, Kent, and he arranged to meet Ron at the factory the next week to discuss a deal for using the factory to produce the fuel tanks.

At the meeting the owner of the woodworking factory discussed the design, building and production of the Spitfire fuel tank with Ron and they agreed to form a limited company together. But they needed another director to raise the amount of money required to start the company. The owner of the woodworking company suggested the owner of several local laundries as a possible candidate. On arranging a meeting with the laundry owner an agreement was reached which provided three directors of the company. Each director put in £333 to form the £1,000 limited company, with Ron becoming the managing director. To get the money to start the business Ron had to borrow from Vi, who made him promise to repay her in one year, which he did after a struggle.

Ron obtained the first order from the Air Ministry for five hundred Spitfire fuel tanks, the start of his first business venture. He moved into a bedsit in Folkestone. Sally then followed Ron to Folkestone to manage the production of the Spitfire fuel tanks, moving into a flat in Folkestone before the couple moved in together. Ron started with a staff of twenty and in a year it grew to a hundred, mainly women. Ron then bought the first partner out after a year for £1,000 and the second partner after three years for £6,000.

Ron remembers transporting the skeleton wooden fuel tanks between his two factories in Folkestone and Dover in an Austin 7 with a trailer on the back to finish the production of the tanks before delivery to the Air Ministry.

Ron was the governor, but he also had other jobs to maintain the production flow for the Spitfire fuel tanks.

On taking a break in a cafe one lunchtime in Folkestone, Ron opened a personal letter addressed to him which he had received that morning. It contained call-up papers asking him to report to the Royal Sussex Regiment in Hastings in ten days' time. Ron promptly drew a line through the letter, wrote "not known" on it and posted it to the return address. He heard nothing more.

After several journeys delivering the wooden skeleton fuel tanks from one factory to the other for completion and painting, Ron noticed a man sitting in a car outside the factory who was obviously monitoring Ron's movements. The man later came into the office and explained that he worked for the Manpower Board and that somebody in the area had reported that Ron's work was not necessary to produce the Spitfire fuel tanks. Ron explained that the contract he had with the Air Ministry to produce the Spitfire fuel tanks was an important part of the war effort because the extra fuel tank enabled the Spitfires to fly further, and the man agreed. Ron then became good friends with the man from the Manpower Board and later employed his son to run one of his factories.

Wanting to expand the business, Ron bought an old building in Dover and a major site in Ashford. The site in Ashford was constructed on a flood plain using concrete road blocks removed by the local council from use as shuttering in the construction of new roads. The business then developed and manufactured metal aircraft fuel tanks and other aircraft components. Then Ron gave up the lease on the factory in Folkestone and sold the Ashford factory to build a larger factory in Dover.

The Spitfire fuel tank contract came to an end after World War Two and Ron had to change direction in his business. He obtained a contract from the government to manufacture new pre-fabricated buildings in his factory at Dover; they were needed to house people left homeless by the bombing raids. This contract continued until all the homes had been delivered, at which time Sally parted from Ron, walking out of the business. The business then moved to producing coach-built coaches, buses, motorised caravans, the name of Ron's new Coachbuilding company was called (Kenex) a name made up from Kent (Ken) and Sussex (ex).

Ron was in the local pub one day when he overheard a conversation in which the initials P and L were mentioned in association with a company tendering for a contract for vehicles. On returning to the office Ron asked his sales staff what the initials PL referred to and one of the salesmen said, "Port of London Authority." Ron immediately phoned up the Port of London Authority, spoke to the buyer and arranged a meeting with him. This meeting resulted in a contract to produce bullion vans for the Port of London Authority at the Kenex factory in Dover.

Another coach-building job the firm undertook was to build additional railway coaches for the Romney, Hythe and Dymchurch fifteen-inch gauge light railway, which was opened on 16th July 1927. It was a miniature public railway running from Dymchurch down to New Romney, which in 1928 was then extended down to Dungeness, making the railway line thirteen and a half miles long. It was a big tourist attraction in the area as well as providing a daily public railway service for local people. The railway line had been requisitioned by the War Office during the war. They used a miniature armoured train to guard the construction of a fuel pipe line under the English Channel called Pluto which supplied the Allied invasion force with fuel. The railway also had several important visitors, including Laurel and Hardy, who opened the new Romney to Dungeness railway section in 1947.

Ron won another contract to provide a new railway on Southport Pier, which was one mile long, and design and supply the train and coaches. This enquiry came via a man

21

Ron had met who worked for the Dover council and who had helped Ron set up his new factory in Dover. Ron project-managed the contract over three months, staying in Southport for this period. While there he increased his interest in playing golf, touring the local golf courses until the contract was completed and fully operational.

The Coachbuilding business, including the staff and stock, was eventually sold to the Martin Walter group, Kenex's main competitor with its Dormobile motor caravans, and the building was sold to Fiat motor company. Ron remembers the anxiety and sleepless nights until the contracts were signed in the back of a Rolls-Royce with Peter Rowley, his solicitor, on the North Circular road in 1960. Ron had now done his first complete business deal, from starting a business from nothing, obtaining contracts and producing the products to the point of sale to make a profit on his investment.

Ron had always been a sportsman, having starting playing football at fifteen for the village team until the war started. In 1940 he joined a team in Folkestone, playing with Wilf Amory, who had previously played professional for Ayr United football club. After a series of footballing accidents, Wilf decided to move to Folkestone to play part time while working for Folkestone Water Company, and he was one of Ron's best friends for many years. Ron's football-playing days came to an end when he broke his leg playing against Worthing with Wilf. Ron was taken to hospital by ambulance and on the way the vehicle got a puncture just outside a pub. Wilf obtained drinks from the pub for the two of them while the driver attempted to change the ambulance's wheel, which took a long time. They had a few more pints before they went on their way. Ron stayed with his mother for the next three months until his leg had healed and he was back to his normal self. This episode ended his football playing days at the age of thirty.

Now, Ron decided that if he could not play for the club, he would go into management. So Wilf became the manager at Folkestone Football Club and Ron became the chairman, and

One mile long Southport Pier Railway

*Romney, Hythe and Dymchurch Railway
Dr Syn Locomotive*

the next ten years he would say were the best of his life. Wilf became a director of the club in 1959, and in 1970 the club had a testimonial match in his honour. Wilf was actively involved with the club until its demise in 1990. The club was now called Folkestone FC and Wilf was invited to become its president, which he did until his death in December 1996. The club has now named its nine-hundred-seater main stand as the Wilf Amory Stand in his memory.

Ron remembers going to the 1966 World Cup Final between England and Germany with Peter Rowley, his solicitor. On driving up to the main gates at Wembley Stadium they found they had nowhere to park Peter's Rolls-Royce and Ron asked the attendant on the gate where to park. Ron then charmed the Parking attendant into providing a parking space for Peters Rolls Royce in Wembley Stadium for which they had no ticket

3 – The Austin and Ford Dealerships

Ron bought Broadmead, a large house in Folkestone, where he lived most of the time to keep his eye on the business. He was now planning his next business move, having obtained an Austin sub-dealership from the main dealer in Folkestone. Ron needed to provide a service workshop and a car showroom, so he bought a building in Shorncliffe Road in Folkestone which was of metal-clad construction and set about building a new brick workshop frontage behind the existing metal frontage with two workshop doors. He then demolished the existing metal frontage to reveal the new brickwork frontage of his workshops. He then obtained a showroom in Sandgate Road by doing a deal with the owner: he met with the opposition who also wanted the showroom over lunch and scuppered their deal by signing the deal with the owner straight after lunch.

Ron had now set up his Austin dealership. But the Austin main dealer then complained to the Austin Motor Company that Ron was "not a suitable candidate and of financial standing to own an Austin dealership" in a letter to Sir Leonard Lord, chairman of the Austin Motor Company. In response Chris Buckley, the sales director, wrote back to the main dealer to cancel their Austin dealership, making Ron the main dealer in Folkestone.

Ron travelled to London to obtain a licence to build a new factory in Dover, and while in conversation with a government officer he learned that Pfizer, a large American company, was going to move into the Folkestone area. The officer thought that Pfizer would possibly need a fleet of cars for its sales representatives. He knew the boss of Pfizer, Richard Fenton, and referred Ron to him.

Richard and Ron met in the Piccadilly Hotel that day and had lunch. During lunch Muddle gained Richard's confidence and he came away from the meeting with a firm order for 20 hire cars. The cars were difficult to get at the time, but Austin Motor Company agreed to supply them to complete the deal.

The day came when the sales representatives were ready to pick up their cars from the dealership in Folkestone. They arrived at two p.m., but the cars had still not arrived. Richard Fenton was not amused, but at half past three the cars arrived on car transporters at the dealership for the sales representatives to collect, which saved Ron's skin.

Orders for more cars came from Pfizer as the company expanded and Ron formed a new company to handle the business. The word got around to other big pharmaceutical companies, which resulted in further orders for company hire cars.

Ron began looking for someone to manage the hire car business. Then his friend, the chief of police, arrived at Ron's office and told Ron that he had retired and was looking for a job. Ron appointed him as manager.

The business grew to eight hundred and fifty cars a year and made large profits for the company for many years. The cars were supplied to the customer on a contract hire facility, whereby Ron purchased the cars and contracted them to the customer over a fixed period of time. The cars then were re-sold at auction by Ron to make a further profit on his investment.

The operation was expanded further by supplying other big businesses in the area with fleets of cars. The salesmen employed by Ron had their own sales areas – new cars, second-hand cars and contract-hire cars – with specialist salesmen with experience designated to each. This created a more professional approach, rather than being a jack of all trades, and made the business more efficient and profitable.

Ron made the Austin dealership very successful, selling a lot of Austin cars and light trucks, but he could not obtain a regular supply of vehicles to keep pace with his sales. So he made an appointment with Chris Buckley, the sales director of Austin, to iron out the problem. Ron arrived on time for the appointment early in the morning in Birmingham, but was not seen by Chris until later in the afternoon, way past the arranged appointment time. Ron made his points known to Chris in no uncertain terms, and said if Austin could not fulfil his requirements, he would be looking for alternative dealerships, such as the Ford Motor Company. Chris, who was about to retire from the Austin Motor Company, then picked up the phone and spoke to someone, and he informed Ron that he had been speaking to the sales director of Ford Motor Company and Ron had an appointment with the director at nine a.m. on Monday at his premises in Ashford. This meeting had provided Ron with a possible manufacturer that could meet his requirements, and it was the market leader worldwide.

During World War Two the Ford Motor Company in England turned its Dagenham production facility over to producing Merlin aero engines and tractor production. The factory suffered regular German bomb raids. After the war Ford introduced a new range of cars, including the Ford Consul and Zephyr Mark I. At the time that Ron was looking at investing in a Ford car dealership, Ford had introduced the Ford Cortina Mark I in England, which became an instant success.

Ron was invited to be guest of honour at a dinner given by the local chamber of trade where he was to give a speech to the local businessmen and he did not have a female companion to accompany him. He talked to a friend, the inspector of licensed passenger vehicles for the area who had visited his Kenex factory. He reminded him of a girl he used to meet at the Leas Cliffe Hall in Folkestone on his nights out who was the ex-girlfriend of the entertainment manager and had since moved to Margate and married. Ron phoned up Joan and invited her to be his partner at the event, which was the start of their romance.

Ron and Joan married in June 1951 at the Ashford registry office with two lady employees of the Registry Office as witnesses.

They took a honeymoon in the south of France, finishing the night of Joan's birthday in a casino. Back in England, Joan sold her small farm and moved in with Ron. The following year, 1952, Caroline was born, and in 1954 along came Richard.

In 1955 Ron's lawyer bought Buxford Farm at auction. It was one hundred and twenty acres and rundown, with a house built in 1600. Originally a water mill, Buxford was operating as a corn mill until just after the Second World War. A water wheel driven by the River Stour stream at the side of the mill had been removed when Buxford was converted into residential use, and there had been failed attempts to run it as a restaurant and hotel. The property been derelict for some time before Ron bought the farm. He contracted a local builder he knew to renovate the house, and after four months the Muddle family, Ron, Joan, Caroline and Richard, moved into the property

Ron then bought Singleton Manor, just up the road. It came with four hundred acres of land. Ron sold off ten acres of his own before he signed contracts, which paid for Singleton Manor. It was a big Tudor house surrounded by a moat; to enter you crossed a bridge over the moat. After buying Singleton Ron went down the local pub to try to get some farm hands and was pointed in the direction of Frank Holyer. Ron went to his house and offered him a job straight away. Ron then also employed Johnny Holyer and his brother-in-law, Joe, and later Dave from the village who worked for him all the years he had Singleton Manor.

Ron also visited his old friend Jack Kealey with whom Ron had grown up in Jarvis Brook. He was the huntsman of the Hambledon Hunt in Hampshire, and a very good horseman. Jack agreed to move to Singleton Manor on his retirement and get involved with the family's horses, the kids' show jumping and the upkeep of Ron's polo ponies. Ron started converting the oast house at Singleton Manor into a flat where Jack and his family could live.

Ashford, in the centre of Kent, was a market town with a

Ron, Richard and Caroline at Singleton Manor

Richard and Caroline outside Singleton Manor when Ron had the Austin Dealer in Folkestone before he changed to the Ford Dealer franchise

Peacocks Ford Dealer in Folkestone - Ron's second Ford Dealership

big railway works that maintained the trains and rolling stock used on the railways running between the coast and London. Ashford was the centre of a planned infrastructure of roads and railways between London and the coast, and so Ron saw it as the ideal place to place a Ford dealership. He could see that Ashford would expand in the future, creating new businesses and housing, which would provide more business for his dealership.

Ron signed the deal for the Ashford Ford dealership with the Ford Motor Company and then designed and built the new Ashford Ford dealership in Beaver Road called County Motors. The building was on two levels, with the workshop on the second, level with the outside road entrance, and the first, in the basement, used for new car storage and a car park. A separate showroom was built at the side of the main workshop to display and sell the Ford car range. The workshops provided the services for Ford products required by the Ford Motor Company and any warranty work required on the vehicles after their sale to the customer

County Motors serviced and repaired Ford cars and trucks from the Ford Anglia, Cortina and Zodiac car range to the Ford Anglia and 400e vans to the Ford Thames Trader trucks manufactured by the Ford Motor Company. The workshop was divided into a car workshop, truck workshop, body shop, paint shop, electrician's shop and stores. The company employed up to thirty skilled motor engineers, body shop panel beaters and painters, all of whom had their own apprentices who were indentured to County Motors and attended the local South Kent Technical College in Ashford on day release.

The cars then were not high-tech as they are today. They had plugs and points ignition, no electronic ignition or fuel injection, and a mechanic needed skill to tune the cars up and set the carburettors and ignition. Later the company made an investment in a "Suntester" for diagnosing and tuning cars.

Also, due to the continual design development of the cars, new skills had to be learnt.

Ford Anglia

Ford Mk 1/Lotus Cortina

Ford Mk III Zodiac Saloon

Over time Ron expanded his Ford dealerships to seven main dealerships in Folkestone, Dover, Deal and Hythe and two garages in Mitcham, Surrey. All the Ford main dealers that Ron owned traded profitably.

The Ford model range changed over the years with the introduction of electronic ignition and electronic fuel injection, which made the cars more reliable and fuel efficient, and other electronic-operated systems like ABS (automatic braking systems), leading to today's cars, which are fully electronically controlled.

The modern workshops also employed up-to-date garage equipment and diagnostic machines to help the motor vehicle technicians service the vehicles in their workshops. The introduction of the mandatory MOT test was another major change in the automotive workshop service. This was a different world to when Ron had started working in his father's garage with a jack and axle stands, working on all makes of vehicles. In addition, the volume of cars on the roads had increased, and now nearly every family owned a car that required servicing and an MOT test by the local garage.

Ron had a good, stable business. Good managers, like George Parker, Ron's company accountant, and Jock, his service manager at County Motors, left Ron more time to pursue other interests with his family, which included horse riding, hunting, polo, golf, skiing, snooker and sailing on his boat, *The Carimuda*.

Ron had been advised by his doctor that he was working too hard and would eventually burn out and suffer health problems if he did not alter his lifestyle. He gave him some very good advice:

"When you get home in the evening, before you have dinner, sit in an armchair and drink a large sherry slowly and then have another one. After your dinner, pour out a large whisky and drink it slowly and then have another one. Now you've stopped for two hours longer and rested." and will have a better lifestyle and try and have a sports interest to keep fit which turned Ron's interest to other sports he could participate in with his friends.

4 – Ron's Life of Leisure and Sports

Ron had grown up and gone to school with Eric Oliver, whose father owned the local coal yard where Eric had worked since leaving school. Eric had started motorcycle grass track-racing as a teenager, with Ron assisting Eric as his mechanic to prepare the bikes for racing and acting as mechanic at the racetracks. Eric had then graduated to solo road-racing and he rode at the Isle of Man Tourist Trophy races before the Second World War. He entered service as a flight engineer with Bomber Command, flying forty missions, and returned to solo motorcycle racing after the war. He later turned his efforts to motorcycle-sidecar racing in the Isle of Man TT's and grand prix circuits abroad.

Eric had always used Norton motorcycles fitted with single-cylinder 600cc and then 500cc engines, and he used a one-off Watsonian sidecar especially developed for road racing. During the 1953–54 season Eric had developed the kneeler sidecar design. Instead of sitting upright on the motorcycle frame, the rider kneeled on a platform. This lowered the centre of gravity and, combined with the "dustbin fairing", which enclosed the rider and provided better aerodynamics resulted in great speed – the same design is used in motorcycle-sidecar racing today.

Eric won four motorcycle-sidecar world titles in 1949, 1950, 1951 and 1953. In the 1960 TT sidecar practice Eric partnered with Stan Dibbden the bolt holding the front forks sheared and they crashed out, resulting in Eric breaking his back in two places (Stan was thrown clear and was not seriously hurt). Both fully recovered and Eric then decided to retire from his successful career in motorcycle racing.

He opened a motorcycle shop in Staines in Middlesex. He was still competing in motor racing, but this time on four wheels instead of three in a Lotus Elan. Eric died as a result of a stroke in 1980, having achieved a lot in his life, reaching

Eric Oliver and Les Nutt winning the
Isle of Man TT in 1954

the top rider position in his sport for which he is still remembered today.

Ron always went to the Isle of Man to support Eric. He remembers flying back from one Isle of Man TT with two friends in a plane that they had hired. On reaching the south coast the pilot turned the wrong way along the English Channel coastline. The planes then did not have the sophisticated navigation systems that they do today and the pilot was lost. Ron, looking at the compass, knew they were going in the wrong direction and he told the pilot to turn around and head along the coast to Lympne Airport just outside Folkestone. But the extra flying time had reduced the amount of fuel that the plane had on board and Ron was getting concerned.

By the time they had reached Lympne Airport, which had a grass runway, it was covered in darkness and they could not see where to land. They radioed the airport flight tower and asked if the ground crew staff could park cars each side of the runway with their headlights on so they could land between the lights. Thanks to Ron's quick thinking, this they managed to do safely, when the plane was nearly out of fuel.

Through his business contacts Ron had met Richard Fenton, the chairman of Pfizer of Sandwich, who introduced Ron and Wilf to playing squash on the local council's squash courts. Richard had been a "Cambridge Blue" at squash and it was wonderful to learn from his experience and expertise.

After about a year the council decided to demolish the squash courts. Ron found out that an acquaintance of his, Don Chaffey, a film producer, had a private squash court in the Alkham Valley just outside Folkestone, and there he continued to play for many years.

One of Ron's cousins who played for the ladies' Kent county team came and played squash with Ron and she could not keep up the pace, which made Ron realise that he had achieved a very high standard in squash.

Ron had already started playing golf and he worked very hard at the game, reaching a handicap of sixteen after three months. He played every Sunday and every first Tuesday in the month for many years. With a good friend, Max Walters, a well-known local businessman, he won the Halford Hewitt foursomes at the Royal Cinque Ports Golf Club. One wet Sunday over a pint with friends Ron was looking at *The Golfer's Handbook* and he found out, to his amazement, that he had played at two hundred and thirty-two golf courses in Europe. To this day he is an honorary member of the Royal Cinque Ports Golf Club.

When Ron moved into Singleton Manor he made it his business to introduce himself to his neighbours, including Arthur Goddard who had a farm just down the road at Chilmington. On meeting Arthur, Ron greeted him with, "I was told you were a difficult old bugger, so I thought I'd better come and meet you."

Something must have gelled after this first meeting between the two of them as they became great pals and played snooker together at Singleton Manor on a regular basis.

Arthur Goddard was involved with hunting in the local Ashford Valley Hunt and he pestered Ron to come hunting with him. Ron was busy with his Ford business, but eventually he gave in. He already had stables at Singleton Manor and now he decided to obtain a hunter that was fit for the job. Before Jack Kealey moved to Singleton Manor on his retirement and the Oasthouse flat had been completed for Jack and his family to live in Ron asked Jack to help find him a Hunter. Jack had a lot of hunting contacts but he said, "Ron, you can't ride." Ron's reply was, "Well, that's my problem."

Later Jack phoned Ron to say that he had found a suitable horse and Ron made an appointment to go and see it. He went down to Hampshire with Arthur to see the horse. The big horse, Paddy, was saddled and Arthur rode it to suss it out. Ron made an offer for the horse of a thousand pounds and the lady owner remarked, "But you have not ridden the horse." Ron then explained that he could not ride but he was going to learn.

Ron still does not know to this day whether he learnt to ride the horse or the horse taught him how to ride, but the two of them made perfect partners. One day, out riding in Godinton Park, Ron bent over to undo a five-bar gate when "the old bugger" jumped the gate from a standstill. Ron never opened another five-bar gate with Paddy in his twelve years of hunting with the Ashford Valley Hunt. The Ashford Valley Hunt met at Singleton Manor once a year and hunted in the fields around Singleton Farm. This was the start of Ron's interest in horses. Caroline and Richard then had ponies of their own and accompanied Ron out hunting, and they also went "hunter trialling" all over the south-east as a family.

Ron also showed an interest in polo, and on returning home one night to Singleton Manor he found a polo pony in his stables complete with ball and polo sticks with a note from Alan Fairbrass, a local stud owner and polo player, that read: "Have left the pony, ball and sticks for you to practice with."

Ron soon got hooked and he bought another polo pony and started playing with a local polo club on a young farmer's field near Canterbury. The club recruited several army officers based at the Dover garrison who played good polo. Everything was going fine until the officers were posted abroad then the farmer suddenly died.

Ron had a few polo players but no polo ground to play on. But he had now got the bug and so he joined the Ham Polo Club, playing two days a week in Richmond Park and at weekends. At the club Ron had a great polo team manager and player, Billy Walsh, who played for the club for many years.

Ron then toured the country with his own team, playing other polo teams and tournaments, which got him noticed by other polo players. One day, after a polo match, Ron met Paul Withers, the English team polo captain, sat in the bar. He talked to Ron about the English team touring Argentina for a month, explaining that a team member had dropped out and asking whether Ron be interested in joining the team. Ron asked for forty-eight hours to decide while he worked out whether he could afford the trip. Subsequently he agreed to Paul's offer and two weeks later he was on the plane to Buenos Aires, Argentina.

On landing at the airport the team were met by officials who drove them twenty miles to a small village, where they had house at their disposal complete with maid, cook and a car. Another team member with Ron was Johnny Mulhern, the Irish polo captain who had married the Irish prime minister's daughter. What a character.

Ron played polo every day. All of the polo ponies were turned out into the fields where there was little or no grass, and then rounded up in a corral so that the riders could take their pick of the ponies for the next polo match. The "grouchos" who looked after the ponies also played to make up the numbers, and they were far better players than any Englishman.

The idea behind the trip was to bring a planeload of polo ponies back to England. Ron travelled one hundred miles north to look at buying ponies. The pony trader gave Ron and Johnny lunch and afterwards the ponies were paraded before them. Johnny rode a couple of the ponies and insisted Ron ride a pony himself, but Ron was not interested. On inspecting the ponies they found they were red hot, possibly due to drugs to make the pony more lively. So Ron was not interested in purchasing any of the ponies and he and Johnny left.

Ron eventually bought six polo ponies to take back to England and the team purchased 32 polo ponies in all. Ron kept two ponies for himself and sold the rest for a very good profit.

Before Ron left Argentina he was invited by the local vet to visit his home two hundred miles south in a small town called Bariloche. He and his wife lived on a 20,000-acre estate. Along with two of the team, Ron hired a private plane

Ashford Valley Hunt Meeting at Singleton Manor

Jack Kealey Huntsman of the Hambledon Hunt lifelong friend of Ron until he died in March 1976

Ron and Richard Cross Country Horse Riding

Ron Playing Polo

and flew to the local airfield near Bariloche. The airfield consisted of a wooden hut the size of a car garage and there was not a soul in site.

Eventually, a workman turned up on the airfield to take Ron to the vet's estate, but he could not speak a word of English so they drove on the tarmac road for five miles in complete silence. The road then turned into a ten-mile rough dirt road until they arrived at a locked gate to the estate. The gate was unlocked and they passed through, the driver getting out to lock the gate again behind them. They then travelled a further three miles on a rough road until they reached the estate.

The house was palatial, and Ron and his teammates were greeted by a beautiful Indian lady who showed Ron to their rooms and told them to use all the hot water they wanted as it was from a natural spring and did not cost anything. They then had a good evening meal and retired to bed.

Ron's host, the vet, returned the next day, and he revealed that they had no meat for food over the weekend. So Ron, the vet and the worker who had driven them to the estate jumped in the vet's Jeep and drove for miles over the estate, looking for something for lunch. They eventually came across a large bullock, which the vet shot. The bullock was tied by rope to the back of the Jeep to be dragged back to the house, but it got stuck in a bog on the way home. The Jeep was up to its axles in mud and could not be moved. The countryside was alive with wild, roaming bullocks, bears, horses and deer. The vet managed to lasso a wild horse, and he told Ron and the worker to start walking in the direction of the house, then he rode back to the estate house for help. Ron and the worker followed the track to the best of their ability, but it was getting dark and it was very frightening being alone in this environment. After walking miles, the vet turned up in a car to take them back to the house.

The following morning they all returned to the site of the grounded Jeep and the dead bullock with two tractors to try to pull the Jeep and the bullock from the mud. In tandem, the two tractors hitched up to the Jeep could not move the Jeep and the bullock. The vet then went home and returned with four large oxen in harnesses and with them he managed to pull the Jeep and the bullock out of the mud. They dragged the bullock back to the lawn in front of the house, where the bullock was cut up and cooked for lunch.

Boy, it was tough!

The same afternoon Ron played a three-a-side polo match on the front lawn. While the game was in progress the largest brown bear that Ron had ever seen strolled across the lawn, totally ignoring the polo match.

Ron and the polo team flew back to Gatwick Airport with their polo ponies after an interesting polo-playing experience which Ron would never forget. On unloading the ponies at Gatwick, Ron found that two of them with his name on were not the ponies he had bought, but it was too late for any recourse and the ponies were now his.

Ron was then invited to captain the Kent polo team to play against the Cambridge University polo team. On arrival at the match, Ron found out that HRH Prince Charles was the captain of the Cambridge University polo team. After an excellent, well-balanced team match in which the Kent team was thoroughly thrashed, the hosts laid down the red carpet for Charles, finding the team drinking tea from a small china cups.

Charles asked, "Ron, where can we get a drink?" Ron replied, "Put your cup down, say nothing and follow me to the beer tent."

Ron had a few pints with the Cambridge team, and he later commented, "You could not find a more sensible conversationist than Charles, despite all the public criticism of him."

One of Ron's other ambitions was to learn to ski. With Joan seven months pregnant, they travelled to London, and after attending to Ron's business at about lunchtime they arrived at the Thomas Cook travel agency. Ron announced to the travel agent, "I would like to go skiing. Where would you suggest I go to ski?" The young and polite travel agent suggested that he should fly to Geneva, from which he would have a good choice of places to go.

The next flight to Geneva was at half past ten the next morning, and Ron offered to pay by cheque. But the agent would not accept a cheque; they took credit card only, which Ron did not use. So Ron jumped into a black cab and went to Portobello Road to see a good friend, Jack, who ran a large cooked meat shop there. Ron had stayed in the flat above the shop when he started work for the Air Ministry and had also helped out in the shop. Ron explained his situation and asked Jack if he could lend him £120 cash to pay the travel agent. Jack was happy to help Ron out, but he explained that his wife had just gone to the shops in London and had taken the safe key with her. Jack could give Ron some notes and the rest in silver.

The silver took over an hour to count out, and then Ron went back to the travel agency to purchase his tickets for the flight the next morning. He had to count all the silver again. It would have been quicker by cheque.

The next morning Ron and Joan flew to Geneva. On arrival at the airport at lunchtime Ron noticed a large poster advertising "Come skiing in Chamonix". Ron and Joan took the bus to Chamonix. It took four hours to reach the Chamonix ski resort, stopping at several other ski resorts on the way, including Megève and St Gervais. Ron and Joan were not dressed for the weather and were frozen stiff.

On getting off the bus Ron asked a passerby in his best French, "Where is the best hotel in the town with good food and accommodation?" Ron and Joan booked into the hotel the local man suggested. The temperature outside at this time was nineteen degrees below zero.

The next morning Ron went to the local bank to change some money and he spoke to the bank manager, a charming man who spoke good English. He asked the manager if he could recommend a small hotel up in the mountains. The manager then phoned a customer of his who had a hotel in the small village of Argentière, seven miles away. The hotel was fully booked that night, but he booked Ron and Joan in for the following day.

The next morning Ron and Joan caught the mountain railway to Argentière. The Hotel Savoie was opposite the station, and standing in the hotel doorway was Mark Carrier, the manager of the hotel, which was a family-run business. Mark, Ron and Joan immediately struck up a rapport, which would turn into a friendship spanning holidays at the hotel over the next eighteen years.

Ron then explained to Mark that they only had booked five days at the resort and he wanted to learn to ski. He did not have any ski clothes, but Mark lent him his spare ski trousers and a pullover and he took Ron to the ski shop to hire some ski boots. Mark phoned a ski guide and instructor called Laurent, and that afternoon Ron joined a ski class along with four lady beginners. Ron, being a bit of athlete, progressed reasonably well, and he arranged a private lesson with Laurent the following morning. After two more days of practice and instruction, Ron was getting the hang of this very difficult sport.

When the time came to go home, Ron promised Mark he would be back the next year, and the following year Ron booked the holiday early, going in late January. Joan had private ski lessons and Ron did his best to ski with the family with Laurent, his personal ski instructor, who over the years became part of the family. On the 3rd Ski holiday Ron then took Caroline, who was then six, and Richard, who was then four, skiing.

On Caroline and Richard's first ski holiday with Ron and Joan, Laurent put on Richard's skies and then Caroline's. He then looked around to see Richard had skied fifty yards down the slope at his first attempt, and as he was responsible for the kids' safety, he dropped everything, skiing after Richard, who was disappearing down the mountain at great speed. Laurent caught up with Richard and stopped him in his tracks, giving him a lecture in French which the boy could not understand in any way. But Ron later made it clear to Richard that he was not to ski without first obtaining the ski guide's okay.

Caroline and Richard subsequently spent many Christmases with Mark's family (which included two daughters of a similar age to Ron's children) and became very competent skiers over the next few years.

One day Ron and his family were on a short break in Hayling Island when they got stuck in traffic on the way home for two hours in Chichester. The next morning Ron swore he would get a boat "to get away from the maddening crowds". Ron had worked extremely hard for long hours to achieve his goals and now he wanted to reap his rewards. By buying a boat, Ron could spend more time with his family.

Ron phoned the commodore of the British Royal fleet, who was a personal friend, and asked for his advice on purchasing a suitable boat. The commodore said he knew a little about small boats and he offered to go to Southampton with Ron, where he was sure that some of his crew could advise him of a boat that would be suitable for his requirements. Ron agreed to pay for the commodore's expenses and to go look at a sixty-four-foot ex-Navy Airforce recovery launch, which was berthed at Southampton. A date was made with the boat's agent to view the boat with Tony, the captain and the commodore.

On arrival Ron found the boat "high and dry", beached on the sand. Ron and the captain went aboard to survey the condition of the boat to estimate a suitable price to be offered for its purchase. A price of £1,000 was agreed by Ron, on the condition that the boat was given a good service to ensure that it was seaworthy before collection.

About a month later the boat was ready for collection, and Ron, Tony and George Parker, Ron's main Ford dealer accountant, who had been in the Royal Navy, motored down to Southampton. They spent the night in a hotel before collecting the boat the next morning at seven a.m. They started up the engines, but then, to Ron's disgust, his crew,

Tony and George, admitted that they had never steered a small boat. So Ron took charge, though he had never steered a boat in his life, manoeuvring the boat into the River Solent. Things went fairly well until the sea started to get rough and George, "the old sea horse", was promptly seasick over the side, then lay prostrate in bed for most of the trip home to Dover. After ten hours at sea, they reached Dover, a very busy port, with cross-Channel ferries coming to and fro. Ron lost his sense of direction, so Tony took over the control of the boat, berthing it in the harbour.

Ron arranged for his draughtsman to provide drawings of the proposed boat conversion, to turn the boat from a Navy vessel into a three-birth boat for his family. He had two of his best carpenters convert the wooden-hull boat, until after a few weeks the boat's design as a pleasure cruiser gradually took shape. The boat had three 100-horse-power diesel engines amidships, a large stateroom aft, guest accommodation in the bow, crew's quarters in the fo'c's'le, one bathroom and a sundeck with awning. The completed boat had a displacement of twenty tonnes, with a maximum speed of ten knots. A motorised tender was also fitted to the boat, for use in going to and from the boat while in harbour. This completed the refit of the boat, which was now ready for use at Ron's pleasure.

Ron's first trip in the now renamed *Carimuda* was to France, around the French canals to perfect his navigation skills. The trip included overnight stops to sample the best restaurants before returning home to Dover.

On a trip to Portugal Ron berthed the boat at Setúbal harbour and went ashore to get some milk. A young man greeted Ron in perfect English, asking, "Can I help you, sir?" This young man was Manuel Ferreira and this first meeting was over fifty years ago, but he and Ron are still close friends to this day.

Manuel's business was then based on one small boat, which he used to service the ships in the harbour with all their supply requirements. His business then grew to include six seagoing tugs and the only four-star hotel in the town. He also bought a private yacht and many blocks of local flats. Manuel became a very rich man. As Ron put it, "I made a few bob in my time, but I was not in his class."

When the *Carimuda* was berthed in Portugal, the boat was in the safe hands of Jonah, an ex-fisherman who worked for Manuel who was employed to maintain the *Carimuda* and to act as the pilot, cook, engineer and deck hand.

Ron had the original three diesel engines replaced with two new Perkin's Diesel Engines and he was hoping to do a test trip on the day he arrived on the boat. But Jonah lent on the taffrail on the port side, which broke, and he fell over the side into the water. Ron was not sure that Jonah could swim, and he pulled off his jacket, jumping into the water to help as Jonah floundered beside the boat. Ron pulled Jonah, with his hat back on, to the boat to live another day. Ron then did a quick trip out of the harbour to test the two new Perkins Diesel engines installed which proved to be fine.

On another trip to Portugal Ron went ashore to pay for the fuel bunkering and everybody on board thought that Ron had returned to the boat and was asleep in his cabin. Ron saw the boat leaving the harbour when he came out of the fuel office. It was two hours later that the crew realised that Ron was not on board. Returning to the harbour, they found Ron at the fuel station in a very ugly mood.

On another occasion Ron was on a trip south, leaving Sines for Villa Nova de Miffontes on the Odimera river As he approached the river entrance, one of the engine propshafts started heating up and vibrating, forcing him to shut down the starboard engine. He knew that he could only enter the Odimera harbour at full tide, as there was a sandbank in the way at low tide. It was therefore important that the boat had its maximum power to enter the harbour. Ron managed to get the top covers off the propshaft with some assistance and he removed the top of the propshaft half bearing and tried the power again. This took the squeal out of the rotating bearing, which enabled the boat to be steered to its anchorage to repair the bearing

Soon after Ron arrived, the local town's dignitary, an old count who lived in a castle overlooking the harbour, sent a message to all aboard to join him to dine with him that evening. So, dressed in glad rags, Ron and his crew were rowed ashore across the river in a nine-knot current. They enjoyed a wonderful evening with their host. The dining hall table was so long that each end of the table had a bell to be rung when all the diners had finished their course. The count told them of the loss of three fisherman the previous week who had been trying to get into the harbour, so Ron knew that he had been extremely lucky getting into the harbour without any repercussions.

The following day Ron left on the high tide for a town called Odimera, some ten miles upriver in the heart of Portugal. It was a beautiful hot day for a lovely trip up the river to his destination, where he berthed at the town quay. The girls on board went shopping while Jonah prepared lunch. Ron and his companions decided it was time for a G and T in the sunshine, which led to more G and Ts before lunch. Ron then decided to check the engines oil levels, opening the hatch to the engine room, but unfortunately he tripped and fell head first through the open hatch into the engine room. Ron came back up through the hatch with a bloody nose and cut eyelid, but fortunately with no major physical damage. The girls returned from shopping for lunch, late as usual, and Ron nearly missing the tide for the trip down the river, but then they continued on their journey. The sun went down very quickly in the early evening, and Ron and his crew had to use the old Aldis signalling lamp to guide their way back to the port anchorage.

A few years later, a harbour berth had been bought for the *Carimuda* in Vilamoura, a new marina in the Algarve from which many an enjoyable holiday was spent on onboard the boat. On arriving at the new marina on the next trip, Ron was informed that Jonah had been taken ill and had unfortunately died. Nobody was on the boat to look after her when they arrived in the bright sunshine. They started to clean the *Carimuda* up for the next trip but it began to rain. It rained for a week without a break and the *Carimuda*'s wooden decks, which had shrunk in the sun, leaked like a sieve. The kids enjoyed themselves riding around in the boat's tender, used to take the crew ashore, but Ron was not pleased with the fact that the boat was leaking and made the decision that enough was enough. He decided to buy a plastic boat, part-exchanging the *Carimuda*.

Ron then visited The Boat Show held at Earl's Court, looking at the plastic-hulled boats that were available to fit his requirements. After sorting through different manufacturer products, Ron decided to purchase a ten-metre boat. The boat was fitted with two one-hundred-and-fifty-horse-power Ford Sabre diesel engines and could cruise at fifteen knots. It was nicely designed, with all the features that Ron required, including hanging davits at the aft of the boat fitted with a rubber dingy to transfer the crew from ship to shore.

On collecting the boat from Lowestoft, Ron's first carefully planned trip was from Dover to Brighton marina, where the boat was then berthed. Ron then set off for Ostend and on to Flushing, or Vlissingen as it is now called, then on to the canals of Holland, Germany and France. Many hundreds of locks were encountered on the trip as they passed through the canals of Holland to the Waal, then into the Rhine with its fast currents and many beautiful barges, and then on to the Moselle, which led into the Canal de l'Est. This canal was the highlight of the trip, with wonderful scenery and enjoyed good food in many auberges and restaurants.

Another trip in the summer holiday period in Spain was with a new guest, Barry Setter, Ron's building manager, who had never been to sea before in his life. The trip from Port d'Andratx to a very safe port at Torrevieja was then followed by a trip down the coast to Cartagena, Aquilas, San José and into the bay of Almería. The boat ran into a storm, hitting some very rough water in the bay. While cruising around Ron tried to find somewhere to berth the boat, but he had to return to the port of Almería. Ron rammed both the engine throttles into reverse, missing the sea wall by inches with a sigh of relief. The boat was tied up to the commercial docks with the help of two very helpful policemen. A rough night was spent on the boat, but the next day they headed for Málaga. They visited Arenal, and eventually left the boat for the winter at Port d'Andratx.

On returning to the boat the following Easter holiday, Ron found the hull thick with seaweed growth. Ron spent many hours with the crew swimming under the hull to remove the seaweed growth with brushes, until the hull was reasonably clean for the trip. Then they headed off to Alicante, Benidorm and Ibiza, which Ron remembers as a "grotty place", and then on to Palma de Mallorca.

The trip was interrupted by a snapped balljoint on the steering, which left Ron at sea with no steering. He managed to get the boat into a small harbour, where a mechanic welded back the balljoint. But on turning into Marbella harbour, the hydraulic steering failed again in a rough sea. Ron obtained a new hydraulic steering unit and replaced it himself. The boat was then left moored in Marbella harbour .

This trip taught Ron that he really needed a bigger boat to negotiate the Mediterranean. He flew home and decided to put the boat up for sale in the *Motor Boat and Yachting* magazine. After several weeks of no interest he received a phone call from a prospective buyer who wanted to view the boat as soon as possible before the end of his tax year in a week's time. Ron agreed to meet the prospective buyer at Gatwick Airport, flying with him to Málaga and then driving to Marbella. On reaching the boat Ron slipped the moorings and started out to sea with the prospective buyer, which was a bit choppy on the day. Ron had fitted a new hydraulic steering unit after his near-miss with the sea wall and to his disgust he now found that he had fitted the hydraulic hoses the wrong way around, so when he turned left the boat turned right and vice versa.

Embarrassed by this mistake, Ron returned to the harbour to rectify the problem himself, which would take a couple of hours. The prospective buyer asked if he could watch while Ron repaired the hydraulic system and Ron agreed. He disconnected and reversed the hoses and bled the hydraulic system to rectify the problem, then they started back out to sea. The buyer was so impressed by Ron's expertise in rectifying the fault that he agreed a price with Ron. On returning to England Ron was given a cheque for the boat in exchange for the ship's papers. This pleased Ron, as he was convinced that the boat was not for him and that he required a bigger boat for his Mediterranean trips.

Ron visited the London Boat Show again, spending several hours looking at different boats. He decided to purchase a forty-two-foot boat which was very expensive and was made in Norwich in Norfolk. The deal was done on the basis that Ron could have the boat that was on the show stand. Ron later travelled to Norwich to collect the boat and his first stop was Dover. He took off for Ostend with some friends on board, and on mooring up he noticed that the rear of the boat had been blackened by the exhaust. Ron contacted the boat's builders and arranged to deliver the boat back to their boatyard for repair. A few weeks later Ron collected the boat from the boatyard and sailed to France, only to find that the rear of the boat was still blackened by the exhaust. The next day Ron set sail back to the boatyard, where they accepted responsibility for the fault with the boat and gave Ron his money back. Ron was now without a boat once more.

By this point Ron had formed a relationship with Christine from Folkestone. He commuted from Folkestone to Southwell on a regular basis before moving to Southwell to live.

Ron then decided to have a boat made to his own specifications. He arranged a trip to Taiwan, where there were hundreds of boatyards that could build a boat to any specification required at the right price. Christine and Ron

The CARIMUDA Ron's 1st boat

Ron's 2nd boat named RAM (Ronald Albert Muddle)

Ron's 3rd boat with Vi and Joan 2 on board at the Ferry Inn

flew out and spent a week looking for a new boat. They visited twenty-two boatyards before deciding on the boat to buy. Ron paid a deposit there and then, and in the next eight weeks he sent the balance required to the supplier of the boat.

The boat finally arrived on the deck of a cargo ship at the Isle of Grain, where Ron and Christine collected it. He took the boat to the Dover docks, and the next morning headed for Le Havre. They then motored on to Amfreville and St Germain in Paris. The port of Notre Dame was a very tricky place to manoeuvre the boat. The boat was then moored alongside a large motor yacht on the starboard side, and Ron left the boat berthed at the port for three months.

On returning to the boat in September, Ron and Christine left Paris for Meux, where they became stuck in a boat traffic jam for four hours. Once out of the jam, they moored just short of their destination for the night, after a shopping trip for French bread for breakfast, and the next morning they proceeded on to Meux. On reaching the harbour they found only one mooring place was available, alongside a half-sunken boat which they had to climb over to reach the shore, and then they found out that this was the beginning of a boat scrapyard. Ron and Christine made friends with the owners of the scrapyard, who were a super French family – kind, hospitable and always happy to have a drink – and they looked after the boat while it was moored in their boatyard.

Ron and Christine then met up with some friends from Paris who had a big country house in Meux, who introduced Ron and Christine to a super restaurant, Le Marinone. There they had the restaurant's speciality of *moules marinières* in a cream sauce, a meal never to be forgotten.

5 – Ron's Other Businesses

The adventures of Ron and his family and friends surrounding Ron's interest in boats continued late into his life, until circumstances beyond his control (explained later in the book) forced him to sell his boat. Ron was still in the Ford main dealer business, which was ticking over nicely with the aid of his good managers, who looked after the daily running of the business, leaving any major decisions to Ron.

On a trip to Portugal Ron berthed his boat in Setúbul harbour, where he met an American who, once he found out Ron was a businessman, offered him a business deal: a shareholding in the largest bonded warehouse in Felixstowe docks. The secured warehouse was a concrete building set in fifteen acres of land that stored goods delivered to the UK by ships from all over the world. It was a stop-over point for importers of goods, or a storage facility for UK suppliers. The goods were not subject to custom duties if they remained stored in the warehouse in transit to another destination. Only when the goods were delivered and sold in the UK would they be subject to custom duties. The bonded warehouse was therefore a no man's land for the importation of goods around the world, and the owner of the warehouse had to meet strict custom requirements. A lot of imported goods came into the country through the Felixstowe port, the largest container port in the UK, so this was a very profitable business and Ron was interested in the proposition.

On returning to the UK, Ron went ahead with the business with the American. But all that glittered was not gold, and Ron ended up in the High Court in London as he was owed money by his partner. It was an expensive business, and Ron's barrister, Derek Bretherton, the number two partner in Linklaters, advised Ron to settle out of court. This Ron did at great expense to himself: he raised the money to "buy the Yank out", taking over the business himself with no partners.

He subsequently turned the business into a great success, and two years later he sold the company. This was Ron's way: buy a business, make it profitable and sell it at a profit, in this case recouping the money that he had to pay out to overcome the obstacle created by the original partnership.

Joan Muddle was invited to visit the Bahamas by a girlfriend who had settled in the Bahamas, marrying a Bermudian called John, a local businessman. On their first day in the Bahamas, John apologised to Ron, saying that he had made arrangements that day to visit Freeport on the Grand Bahama island to buy some property for letting out. Ron replied, on the spur of the moment, that he would like accompany John to Freeport, and John agreed. On arrival they went to the estate agent's and then they went to look at some semi-detached bungalow properties with the agent. John agreed to buy six of them.

In conversation with Ron, the estate agent mentioned that he had a small business for sale at a good price as the owner wanted to sell up to return to the States. On viewing the business, which was a rundown haulage company, Ron paid a small deposit and said he would return in three weeks to complete the deal. A month later when he returned to the Bahamas, Ron decided to stay on for a month to sort out the business. He had a gut feeling that he had bought a business with potential, but a clause in the contract stated that half the workforce had to comprise black Jamaicans.

The business prospered under Ron's leadership, and he found that the workers were good and spoke English well. One day Ron asked a staff member to go and collect an important parcel from the airport. He later returned and said, "There weren't no parcel, master." Ron then jumped into the van with his employee and drove to the airport. On arriving at the airport warehouse, Ron found the parcel he required sitting inside the door of the warehouse. By law, he needed the correct paperwork to be able to collect the parcel. Ron then trained his staff in the correct procedure for the collection of parcels from the airport by having the correct

Felixstowe Docks is the largest Deep Sea Ship "Container Port" in the UK and can handle the largest Container ships with rail and truck transport delivery services

Container ship at Felixstowe Docks being unloaded at the port

paperwork so this would not happen again.

Ron then bought a house in Freeport and travelled to and fro for seven years from England to Freeport, relying on his office manager to run the parcel business correctly in his absence. The business grew very fast and Ron obtained contracts with British Airways and other airlines using the airport and also set up business links with the shipping lines.

Ron then appointed a London lawyer and an accountant who had offices in Nassau. The accountant, Peter Evans, was a good sportsman and Ron played golf with him quite often.

Ron's lawyer, Peter Rowley, had married a very rich lady called Ethnea and they owned a large house in Folkestone. Ethnea phoned Ron one day to ask if she could come out and stay with Ron in Freeport so that she could see the property she owned in Freeport.

When Ethnea arrived in Freeport, Ron met her at the airport and drove her to her property. They drove down tarmac roads which then became a rough track for a few miles. Ron finally stopped and refused to drive Ethnea any further, saying that any property in this area was worthless. Not believing Ron, Ethnea contacted her estate agent, who confirmed that "Muddle was right". Ethnea stayed a few more days and then flew back home to England.

Ron's next visitor was the famous jockey Lester Piggott, whom Ron knew well. He told Ron that he was thinking of buying a row of twelve detached houses in Freeport. Ron drove Lester to the housing site and inspected one or two of the houses, then told Lester that "he had been sold a pup" and they were worth nothing. The plots contained old cars in overgrown grass and rubbish was piled nearly as high as the roofs. Lester then checked with his estate agent who confirmed that "Muddle was right", so for the rest of the week Ron and Lester played golf until Lester flew home, very disillusioned over his proposed investment

While working in the Bahamas Ron visited the casino most Saturday nights. The casinos attracted the Americans when top-class artists such as Bing Crosby, Frank Sinatra and

Sammy Davis Jr performed there. After the acts had performed their spot, gambling took place on every table in the casino, with the Americans gambling away the night and losing many dollars, while Ron headed home, not gambling at all.

The United Kingdom then decided to grant independence to the Bahamas, which had been under British jurisdiction for years. On one of Ron's visits after the declaration of independence his offices were invaded by local immigration authority personnel. Later the local police arrived and arrested Ron, who was taken into custody, held for several hours and then released after being interrogated.

Ron quickly decided that with the new regime in power this was not the place for him, and he put the business up for sale. It was quickly sold to a Bahamian who paid two-thirds of the price agreed upfront, with Ron lending him the balance to be paid back over five years. Ron's friends were very sceptical about this deal, saying that he might not obtain the full amount that had been agreed. But to everyone's amazement, Ron received his full payment over the next five years, making a profit on the business sale.

At the same time Ron sold his house in the Bahamas and packed his bags to leave. He took the company car, a Ford Drophead Coupé, and motored off to West Palm Beach and then on to Orlando. He spent three days at Disneyland and then drove on to Jacksonville and "turned left" to continue his journey across the southern states of America to the west coast. In Las Vegas he met up with his old footballing friend Keith Denver, who had emigrated to the States, and he sold the Ford to him. Ron then flew back to England in grand style on Concorde: one of the most amazing flying experiences of Ron's life.

Because of Ron's involvement in the building of his early factories in Ashford and Dover, he decided that next he would try his hand at property development. First he bought a very large house in Lower Sandgate Road in Sandgate, Folkestone. He then obtained planning permission to demolish the house to build fifteen apartments with four penthouses, one of which Ron lived in for several years after their completion. During the building work Ron turned up early at seven a.m. one morning to find out that his building manager had been stealing building materials from the site. He sacked him on the spot and promoted a young man called Barry Setter, also working on the site, to manager. Barry worked for Ron in this capacity for the next nine years. On completion, all the properties were sold, but it was not as profitable a deal as Ron was used to. Ron then bought twelve partially derelict flats from the local council in Sandgate. Barry and his crew refurbished the flats to a very high standard and Ron let them out.

Singleton Manor was also run as a business. Ron had a herd of Friesian cows that produced milk for the Milk Marketing Board, using part of the four hundred acres as their pasture. The rest of the land was turned over to the production of corn. The corn had to be harvested every year, which was a highlight in the farm's yearly work. The milking was done at Buxford, where a milking parlour had been set up, and silos were built in the barns to store the corn cut in the field with Ron's German Claas combine harvester. Some of the locals helped out with harvesting the crops, loading the straw bales onto the tractor and trailers to be transported back to the farm for storage.

Ron still had his small agricultural business, which he had set up after the war, based in Ashford, which supplied the farm's Fordson tractors and Claas combine harvester. He remembers a trip to the East German Republic to purchase some farm machinery for his business in 1946 as part of a business delegation from the local businesses in the Kent area. Crossing to East Germany, beyond the dividing wall, was to be one of the most frightening experiences of Ron's life. He was faced with armed guards and guns everywhere. The East German who met Ron took the trade delegation to a large supermarket, which was devoid of any edible goods. Ron commented, "It would have been more appropriate to bring food rather than money." Ron purchased four large trailer fertilizer distributors for £100 each, including delivery to the United Kingdom, and he could not wait to get out of East Germany to return home.

The Ford dealer motor businesses were still going strong, requiring little input from Ron, so he could get involved with other business interests and enjoy life as his doctor had advised. Ron's lifestyle had changed from total work to mixing work with pleasure. The next fifteen years went very quickly as he spent weekends with the kids at horse shows, cross-country riding, indulging his interests in polo and golf.

Then Lucy and Wally, who looked after the house, retired and then Ron and Joans lives changed. The house was no longer harmonious, and disaster struck. Caroline was now working as a secretary at Lympne Airport. One weekend she complained about a pain in her thigh. Ron massaged her thigh, dismissing it as nothing serious, but the next weekend the pain had returned and was much worse. Ron telephoned a surgeon he knew who was on duty at the local hospital and he told Ron to bring Caroline in right away. He examined Caroline's leg and had it X-rayed. Then the surgeon confronted Ron and said, "She's riddled with cancer and won't live more than three months." Caroline was only eighteen years old.

Ron knew that time was precious, and he went out and bought Caroline a Triumph Spitfire Coupé sports car and arranged for a single woman friend, Joan, to accompany Caroline on a tour of France. Eight weeks later Caroline returned to hospital.

When Caroline passed away Ron was devastated. No amount money or success could replace her, and the sorrow has lived with him for the rest of his life. The loss altered Ron's life completely, leading to his divorce from Joan and the sale of Singleton Manor and Buxford Farm, where Vi was now living. Ron sold his Ashford and Mitcham Ford dealer businesses to John Willment – another Ford dealer who was involved in motor racing and was a partner in the

Ford GT40 team with John Wyer, winner of Le Mans in the 1960s.

The other Ford businesses were also sold over a period of time, so ending Ron's involvement in the motor trade business, which had been his life.

Richard stayed with his mother, Joan, until Singleton Manor was sold. The house was sold with planning permission to build houses on the four hundred acres of farmland, which resulted in the expansion of Ashford as an "overflow area" for London. They got a good price for Singleton Manor with its farmland. Joan then bought a property just down the road from Singleton Manor at Chilmington Green, where she lived for a number of years until retirement, when she sold the property and moved in with Richard who bought his own property near Guildford in Surrey.

Vi moved back to Crowborough to live, and Jack and his family moved to a rented house in Kingsnorth.

Ron left Ashford, moving to Fairwarp in Sussex, where he lived for seven years with Joan 2 playing polo three days a week. Ron then moved to the penthouse in Sandgate near the beach in Folkestone. Vi, Ron's mother moved to live in one of the flats at Riviera Court Sandgate for many years until the end of her life at one hundred and two years of age.

Caroline Muddle 1952 – 1970 Aged 18

6 – Lingfield Park Racecourse

When Richard had left school at sixteen, he had wanted to pursue a horse-racing career. But Ron wanted Richard to have a trade behind him, so he arranged a job for his son at an engineering company in Tunbridge Wells called Stormont Engineering, a Ford main dealer. Richard then worked at the Humber Hillman car factory in Coventry, and once he had completed his mechanical apprenticeship, Ron then arranged for Richard to start a jockey apprenticeship.

Richard started work as an apprentice jockey at Middleham, Yorkshire, with Ken Payne. Richard's first race win was on the flat at Catterick. In the paddock Richard was told by his trainer to "jump out of the stalls, smack the horse hard on its backside three times, then forget your whip and ride to the finish all the way without looking around". Richard followed his trainer's instructions and won the race. Ron had gone to Catterick with his friend Sam Rocket, the second man to swim the English Channel. He had placed a bet on Richard to win, and had asked Ron how much he wanted to bet on the race. Ron had said, "Oh, the same as you." After the race in the winner's enclosure, amid all the hugs kisses and handshakes, to Ron's amazement Sam handed him a wad of notes totalling £3,600. He had bet on the horse from twenty-five-to-one down to five-to-two favourite. Richard then transferred to Staff Ingham at Epsom. Unfortunately, Staff Ingham died and Richard then finished his jockey apprenticeship with John Dunlop at Arundel.

Richard went to Cyprus to continue his racing career, winning the Cyprus Derby. Richard was also a guest of the French racing authority at both Arc and Trotting racecourses. The sand track at Trotting inspired Ron and Richard to look into the possibility of all-weather horse-racing in England.

Ron and Richard then flew to Miami, Florida, to look into this further, as America had mostly all-weather race tracks, and they came to a decision to buy an English racecourse and invest in the first all-weather race track in England. Ron met an estate agent in London who informed Ron that Lingfield Park Racecourse was for sale for £1.3 million. Ron said he would consider the proposition and get back to the estate agent. Later he phoned the estate agent and offered £750,000, but he was not taken seriously. A year later, in November 1980, the estate agent moved down from £800,000 and accepted Ron's £750,000. The purchase of Lingfield Park was completed that month and Ron started work on the all-weather equitrack.

The all-weather racecourse was frowned on by the racing community, which did not approve of a commoner's involvement in horse-racing circles and the introduction of an all-weather track. Ron had a meeting with the current course manager, Rod Fabricon, and told him that the first job was to drain the racecourse of surface water. Rod explained that this had been tried before, but had not worked. Ron confirmed that drainage contractors were moving in the next week to start the job. Rod's reply was: "If they do, I'll leave." Ron thanked Rod for his notice and told him to take his foreman with him, which he did – to Goodwood Racecourse, where he stayed for many years. The drainage contractors completed the job successfully and planning permission was then obtained to develop the racecourse.

Ron spent a few days getting to know his staff, learning and listening. He sold off various parts of the land and buildings around the racecourse to fund his expansion plans, which included new private boxes, a large rooftop restaurant in the main stand and an eighteen-hole golf course. Ron also wanted to alter the flash stewards' room to create extra office space for his staff, cutting the room in half to provide the extra office space required and leaving just enough room for the stewards.

Lingfield Racecourse had been owned by one family for ninety-two years, and was run as a hobby, not a business. It was only open for horse-racing when the hunting, fishing and

Richard Muddle on his first professional jockey race ride win at Catterick Racecourse

*Richard Muddle on Pals Bambino winner of the Craven
stakes at Goodwood Racecourse in 1975*

shooting seasons had finished. It was for a Lingfield society clientele, and not for the general public, and therefore it did not make a profit. But Ron was going to change all of this by running the racecourse as a business.

First, Ron phoned Richard, who was still racing as a jockey in Cyprus and was in a bar in Nicosia, and said, "Come home. I've bought Lingfield Racecourse and I want you to run it." Richard flew home to England. Ron then recruited his bank manager, Mac Wale, who had just retired, to show Richard the ropes and teach him about business and organisation.

Mac was fundamental in forming the team at Lingfield, which ran under the name Ram Racecourses Ltd. Mac was also involved with the purchase of Lingfield Park, which had to be verified by the Jockey Club in London. An appointment was made with the Club to explain Ron's intentions in the development of Lingfield. Ron and Mac attended the meeting at 42 Portman Square, London, at nine thirty a.m. At ten twenty-five they were ushered into the office, where no excuse was offered for keeping them waiting. Mac presented the facts to the Jockey Club, explaining that Lingfield was a prestigious racecourse and that its new benefactor, Ron, would fulfil the racecourse's potential by installing the all-weather racetrack, the first one in England. But on returning to the racetrack, the general feeling was there had been a "negative vibe" at the meeting. The racecourse would open using the existing grass and dirt tracks until an agreement could be reached with the Jockey Club to install the all-weather racetrack. Ron owned the racecourse for a further eight years, during which time it always made a profit. He also introduced the Lingfield Derby, which produced several Derby winners.

One of the highlights at Lingfield was his Vi's one hundredth birthday. Ron invited his mother's friends from Crowborough and hired a coach to bring them to Lingfield for a surprise birthday party in the rooftop restaurant. Peter O'Sullevan, the BBC commentator, asked after Vi when

Vi Muddle on her 100th birthday party at Lingfield Park 1988

Vi muddle on her 100th birthday driving Ron's car for the BBC

talking to Ron.

Ron replied, "She's fine and is still driving at a hundred." Peter asked whether Vi would drive a car to be shown on the BBC racing coverage. Vi agreed and drove Ron's car out of the racecourse to the main road and back into the racecourse, and footage was shown by the BBC.

Lingfield Park was then granted permission to install the all weather race track the only one in England at this time and now had become very successful and profitable even though the all weather racetrack was not completed under Ron's ownership.

Ron was approached by two brothers who agreed to buy Lingfield from Ron for seven million pounds in 1990. The deal was completed and Ron looked for his next business venture.

7 – Southwell Racecourse

Ron had now "learnt the racecourse business" and so he looked at buying another racecourse, Southwell. He took a trip to look over a possible purchase of the racecourse, and decided to buy the racecourse along with an additional ten acres of land. But he found out later that the racecourse was owned by a limited company with several shareholders. Ron's accountant sorted out how much money was payable to each shareholder to buy out their shares and obtain control of the racecourse. On payout day an elderly lady who was paid £1,500 gave Ron a hug and a kiss as all the time she had held her shares she had not been paid a dividend and she was extremely pleased to get some money back for her shares.

The travelling up from Folkestone in Kent to Southwell on a regular basis was no fun for Ron, with all the driving involved, so after a few months Ron stayed in the local pub near the racecourse. This gave him more time to plan the development of the racecourse and to get to know the staff, who were pleased to know that the new owner had a positive plan of action, confirming where they stood with their jobs.

After a time the local pub at which Ron stayed went broke. Seeing that the local community wanted a pub, Ron bought The Crown pub and built an extension containing six rooms for bed and breakfast. Ron then employed a manageress to run the business and the pub became a good meeting place, which Ron then sold for a small profit once it was up and running.

After Ron completed the purchase of Southwell Racecourse, on closer inspection what he had bought became clear. The course had a small grandstand and some semi-derelict buildings. The stable lads' canteen and accommodation required work. The grandstand was re-designed and the all-weather racetrack was completed as a perfect oval. This construction was similar to the work carried out at Lingfield, but on a smaller scale.

In 1992 Ron asked Christine to join him at Southwell and she moved there to live with Ron in the old mill house next to the racecourse, which he had bought and converted.

HRH Princess Anne opened the racecourse in 1992, and there was a record attendance of fifteen thousand people on the opening day. Ron then began construction of a mile-long entrance road to the racetrack to make it easier for the public to access the racecourse. In addition, three American-type barns were constructed to enable horses to be stabled and trained at the track.

Once all the racecourse buildings and the new equitrack had been completed and opened to the public, an eighteen-hole golf course was constructed. Nine holes were built in the centre of the racetrack with the other holes constructed on land adjacent to the old mill house where Ron and Christine lived.

Ron had taken a lot of flak from people in high authority in horse-racing circles for his investment in the all-weather racecourse, but he had proved them all wrong, making the all-weather racecourse profitable.

8 – Wolverhampton Racecourse

The former Tote chairman Lord Woodrow Wyatt said of Ron in his biography: "They don't like this Muddle because he is a commoner, but I am certain he will prove them all wrong." Ron also introduced horse-racing over jumps on the all-weather track, but they proved to be a failure; the track was only suitable for flat racing.

Soon after Ron purchased Southwell Racecourse he was approached by a shareholder of Wolverhampton Racecourse, who asked whether Ron would be interested in purchasing Wolverhampton. Ron agreed to attend the next board meeting at Wolverhampton, where the shareholder put forward Ron's plans to completely demolish the existing Racecourse and redesign the racecourse to include an all weather floodlight racetrack, but the motion was not carried by the majority of the shareholders as one shareholder had had joint control of the shares.

One month later the majority shareholder contacted Ron and said if Ron could put his offer in writing before the following Saturday, he was now confident that the deal would be accepted. Ron arranged to meet him at a pub on the North Circular road. The deal was done for Wolverhampton Racecourse, subject to contract, in the back of a Rolls-Royce owned by Peter Rowley, Ron's lawyer in the pub car park. It was 1993 and Ron had completed the deal for Wolverhampton in his seventy-seventh year.

For many hours Ron discussed with Richard the proposed development of the racecourse. Ron then applied for planning permission to build houses on part of the land and, once obtained, he sold the land for development, allowing him to raise money to develop the track itself. Work began on the building of the new racecourse, with an investment of £14.5 million, to include a forty-bedroom hotel and the first floodlit all-weather racetrack in the UK. They had to demolish everything on the site to build the new racecourse, and a new fibresand surface all-weather racetrack that ran alongside the turf racetrack.

Richard became the course manager, and they were very fortunate to have Her Majesty Queen Elizabeth open the racecourse in June 1994. Ron and Christine sat each side of the Queen, watching the racing. The Queen's horse came second in its race, and she very much enjoyed the racing, which drew huge crowds. Afterwards Ron received a letter from the Queen thanking him and his team for an enjoyable and successful day in the Black Country.

Wolverhampton Racecourse became the most successful racecourse in England in its time because of the investment in the all-weather racetrack and the floodlighting of the track, which allowed for horse-racing at night. It became a central business meeting place and entertainment centre for all the community, and it drew riders and runners from around the world, with extensive race coverage on television.

The all-weather racetracks introduced by Ron Muddle were now here to stay, and other racecourses, such as Kempton in 2006, followed the trend, as they realised that this was the future of horse-racing and profitable racetracks.

Ron and Her Majesty Queen Elizabeth II at the Opening of Wolverhampton (Dunstall) Racecourse in June 1994 Ron was in his 78th year and still involved in business

The Wolverhampton (Dunstall) Racecourse Grandstand and All Weather Track with Floodlights around the track for Night Racing

9 – Retirement to the Country

In 1999 Ron and Richard decided to sell Southwell and Wolverhampton Racecourses to Arena Leisure, and Ron also sold the old mill house next to Southwell racecourse where he lived. He moved back south with Christine to his home county, Sussex. They moved into a cottage in Ditchling and Ron took up his interest in golf at the local Mid Sussex Golf Club. The gentleman who had built the club could not make it pay after eight years in business, so Ron decided to buy it.

After a couple of years of living in Ditchling, the cottage behind came up for sale and Ron and Christine decided to buy it. They moved into the cottage, which had stables for horse livery, a barn with an exercise area for horses and several railed paddocks outside. Christine had her own horses in the stables and the other stables were let out to owners who wanted to stable their horses on site. The horses were looked after by Carly a groom and Mark, a professional jockey, who lived on site over the stables and rode Ron's racehorses. Ron and Christine's horses were now trained at Brighton by Sheena West and were raced at Plumpton Racecourse, just down the road, and other racecourses across the country.

Ron and Christine also had two dogs for company in their cosy environment, one light-tan crossbred Alsatian called Kate, and a little black-and-white-coated Jack Russell called Pete from the RSPCA.

After Ron had owned the golf club for two years, he decided to sell it as he had made a good profit (though the previous owner had lost half a million pounds the year before Ron bought the club).

The business world was changing and one of the things that had changed was the fact that you could not just sack people when required: you had to follow a legal procedure. Ron commented, "How can you run a business without sacking people?" This made Ron's decision to sell the Golf Club business when he had made his profit and he was still involved in business deals well into his nineties.

Ron and Christine settled into their new life together, away from the racecourses, although Ron still maintained an interest in horse-racing still having his own race horses. He was enjoying life, with plenty of other things to do in his life including world travel.

Ron had enjoyed his achievements and his meeting with the Queen, but most of all he enjoyed the thrill of the chase, turning the next business around and making a profit. As Ron saw it, this was his job as a wheeler and dealer: to buy it right, work hard and sell it at a profit. He was now in a position where he did not need the money, but had fun doing the business.

Everything was going fine until Ron was in a builders' yard collecting building materials for the cottage in 2001. A fork-lift driver reversed instead of going forward, and he ran over Ron's foot, taking two toes and the flesh off his left foot. Ron had several operations afterwards to try to repair the damage and he spent a year in and out of hospital. After leaving hospital he said, "I am now back at peak form now," but he had to use crutches. He then bought an electric four-wheel buggy to get around the farm to oversee what was going on.

On a trip to Spain to sell his latest boat, soon after Ron's accident, Ron and Christine were transported by buggy from the plane to the airport terminal. Outside the airport terminal the buggy driver said Ron would have to walk the rest of the way into the terminal himself, despite his injuries. Ron was not happy and made his objections clear to the buggy driver in no uncertain manner.

After Ron had sold his last boat he returned home with Christine and starting planning their future around their common interest in horses. Ron still had several racehorses, including Mr Muddle, which had won several times at Plumpton and other racecourses across the country. Christine wanted to breed horses and raise them at home, ready for racing. Ron had owned many racehorses in his life, buying his first horse, Joe Grace, on recommendation from his vet, Arnold Crowhurst, from Eddie McNally, a race horse trainer. Ron ran Joe Grace in a selling race, and it won – it was the only horse to finish the race. That is when Ron got the horse-racing bug. Arnold then told Ron of a customer who had a three-year-old horse on the Romney Marsh. Ron went to view this horse in the driving snow and bought the horse for £300. The horse was called Kentish Pride and it won many races. Other racehorses Ron bought after this were Court Circus, Pals Bambino, Big Pal and Ladbrooke Leisure. The most expensive racehorse Ron bought was Cumbernauld for which he paid £12,000. It was bought on Ron's behalf by Captain Ryan Price and was ridden by, amongst others, Lester Piggott, who won many big races on Cumbernauld. Over time these horses gave Ron a total of thirty-four race wins.

Christine and Ron then bred several racehorses at home, the first being Spatham Rose in 1999, followed by Just Josie in 2006, Nom de le Rosa in 2007, Mr Muddle by Imperial Dancer in 2007, Jack in 2009, Freddie in 2011 and Lacey in 2011. The most successful of these racehorses was Mr Muddle, which had several race wins and was pictured with Ron and Christine when it won at Plumpton Racecourse.

Mr Muddle Ron and Christine's Racehorse winning at Plumpton Racecourse

Mr Muddle Ron and Christine's Racehorse winning at Plumpton Racecourse in the Winners Paddock

10 – World Travel

Ron's foot disability had not stopped him enjoying life with Christine, who shared common interests with Ron. They enjoyed each other's company, making a good team, and still travelled the world to places they had never visited.

In March 1998, before Ron's accident, Ron and Christine had travelled to India, flying from Gatwick Airport and stopping for two hours in Bahrain before landing in India at Goa Airport. They took a taxi to their hotel, with Ron commenting, "The Indian taxi drivers are mad." After booking into the hotel, they had a swim in the pool before eating a meal. A bit hesitant about what to eat or drink, they both tucked into Indian samosas with Tandoori chicken before going to bed and sleeping for over twelve hours to recover from the jet lag.

The next day they took a taxi to the airport and caught a plane to Bombay, having a meal of roast chicken with rice on the plane. There followed another hair-raising trip by taxi; this time they saw cow lying in the busy Bombay road. They arrived at the Taj Mahal hotel, which was luxurious. Ron had a panic about the hotel tickets, but it was all sorted out. They then relaxed with a delicious Darjeeling tea and at dinner had an Indian mixed curry. They took a walk outside the hotel, but they were hustled in the street by the locals, so they quickly returned to the hotel for the night.

Through a third party Ron had already been in contact with the Royal Western India Turf Club, which was aware of Ron's visit. Ron and Christine were invited to the races at Mahalakshmi Racecourse in Bombay by the chairman of the Club, Dr Cyrus S Poonawalla. A huge limousine collected Ron and Christine from the hotel to take them to the racecourse, where they were greeted by Dr Poonawalla, who invited them to lunch. Ron was treated like a celebrity and was invited to present the winner's trophy at the big race of the day. Ron and Christine were then invited to a trainer's stables, where the racehorses were paraded in front of them. After a Chinese meal with the trainer and his wife, they returned to their hotel in the limousine. Ron and Christine really enjoyed their day at the races.

After packing and resting the next morning, they had a meal in the rooftop restaurant before going to the airport to fly to Jaipur, known as the pink city of Rajasthan since a lot of its buildings are painted in a pink hue. There, they booked into their hotel for the night. At nine a.m. the next morning they were collected from the hotel and driven a few miles into the countryside to visit a magnificent amber palace. There, lots of coaches and visitors were surrounded by beggars and elephants.

They then took a five-hour coach trip the next day to Agra and saw lone Indians on the route, sitting on their haunches and meditating in the sun. On the way to Agra a planned stop with a guided tour was taken to visit the Fatehpur Sikri, a deserted red sandstone city that was built Emperor Akbar in the sixteenth century. The city was abandoned over three hundred years ago when the local water wells went dry, and it remains in the same condition today as it was three hundred years ago.

On reaching Agra and booking into their hotel, Ron and Christine met a guide who took them, at sunset, to the Taj Mahal, the monument built to love and devotion that people visit every day. They found the Taj Mahal to be a beautiful, peaceful place.

The guide collected Ron and Christine the next morning for a further visit to the Taj Mahal in the morning sun. On reaching the Taj Mahal they were surrounded by many beggars and boys with stalls trying to sell cards, films and trinkets. Ron and Christine walked around the beautiful gardens, which run alongside a river tributary from the River Ganges. Joining a stream of visitors, they then entered the Taj Mahal to see all the semi-precious stones inlaid in the marble block construction in beautiful patterns, a skill known

Ron and Christine outside the Taj Mahal

Ron and Christine on an Indian Elephant ride

Indian Trained Racehorses shown to Ron and Christine

as pietra dura. They saw the tomb of King Akbar's wife, who conceived sixteen times and died at the age of thirty-nine, and the king's tomb, lying beside his wife in perfect symmetry.

For two days Ron had not felt on top form. Their guide took Ron and Christine to the local American hospital so Ron could get medicine for his sore mouth. On the way back from the hospital they visited a factory that produced beautiful coloured stones to be inlaid in marble-topped tables, plates and boxes.

Ron and Christine then went to visit a palace outside Jaipur and they were transported to the palace up a steep hill on the back of a large elephant. They walked around the palace and were transported back by Jeep. They then went back to Jaipur city and had a meal in another palace. Afterwards they walked around the city, which was bustling with cows, camels, rickshaws, bicycles, beggars and goats, everything under the sun. They saw some Indian carpets being made and printed, and bought some. They then passed the king's palace but it had started to rain, so they went back to the hotel. In the evening they went out for a curry in the city.

At eight a.m., the next morning Ron and Christine left Jaipur for Agra. They had a very interesting car ride through the Indian countryside, seeing camels pulling wagons of wood, sheep and goats being looked after by young girls, and women wearing brightly coloured red and yellow saris. They passed through many villages, which had plenty of shopping places for the locals, and ended up at Agra where they did more sightseeing before returning to their hotel in Jaipur.

They then caught an express train from Jaipur to Delhi a big, old-fashioned, solid train. On arrival at Delhi at ten a.m. they booked into the Oberon Hotel, a very smart hotel in New Delhi, a very prosperous place. Ron was still not feeling on the top of the world, so they cancelled their tour arranged for the day. Instead, they accepted an invitation to a view a stud farm owned by Pradeep Mehra, whom they had met at the races. His was one of the largest stud farms in India. They had a very good day out, but Ron was still feeling rather delicate.

Ron and Christine flew from Delhi to Bombay the next day, then on to Goa, arriving in the afternoon. They were relieved to have arrived, as they had enough of flying all over India, but at least they had seen a lot of India and experienced the different cultures. At Goa they relaxed and Ron felt much better after getting some pills from the doctor. They walked along the beach, where the water was very warm, the sun was hot and there was a nice breeze, and after a half a mile walk they stopped at a sea shack and had a drink of lime with soda and some food before returning to the hotel for a rest. The evening finished with a meal outside the hotel on the balcony, where they enjoyed a meal of white fish with sauce and vegetable fried rice.

Ron and Christine woke early the next day as they had booked a trip to see the dolphins. At eight a.m. they went up the river in a little boat, and after about half a mile they were taken out to sea to join the fishing boats. They saw glimpses of the dolphins when they came up for air: small silver dolphins, bottle-nose dolphins and some brown dolphins with fins. They decided to take another boat across the river to see all the fishing boats, then they went back to the hotel where they met two Scots, Larry and Elsie, who had been there for three weeks and had thoroughly enjoyed their visit to India. Ron and Christine had their best meal yet that night. Ron tucked into two tiger prawns six inches long and Christine had pomfret with fried vegetable rice.

Ron and Christine then travelled to a nearby town on a wild goose chase looking for a curtain shop. In the afternoon they had a really interesting ride through the countryside, stopping at a fishermen's village and giving sweets to the waiting children. They saw mats and rope being made from coconut fibre, then visited a prehistoric cave on a nearby farm. They finished off the day with a meal of more tiger prawns, before retiring to their hotel for the flight back to England the next morning.

Ron and Christine's next holiday adventure was to Peru in September 1999. They flew from Birmingham Airport to Amsterdam where they transferred to another flight to Lima in Peru. The journey took nearly fifteen hours with a stopover in Aruba. On landing at Lima they booked into the Jose Antonio Hotel, and the next morning they returned to Lima Airport for a one-hour flight to Cusco. The skies were cloudy, but they arrived safely at Cusco, the capital of the Inca empire.

They booked into the five-star Libertador Hotel for four nights. The hotel was originally a palace, built by Francisco Pizarro, the conqueror and first governor of Peru, who built the Casa de las Cuatro Bustos as his own palace, using walls and foundations built by Inca labourers. Today, this palace is the two-hundred-and-fourteen-room Libertador Hotel, with modern comforts and the ambience of a Peruvian colonial hotel.

After a much-needed rest, Ron and Christine enjoyed a sightseeing tour of Cusco, visiting the city's beautiful plazas and churches, before travelling to the nearby Inca sites of Tambomachay, Kenko, Puca-Pucara and the impressive fortress of Sacsayhuaman which overlooks Cusco.

After a buffet breakfast they drove to Urubamba, visiting the traditional street market in Pisac where they bargained with the street vendors, before heading through the sacred valley of the Incas. The visit included visiting the quaint streets of the town of Ollantaytambo, an Inca fortress. Then they returned to the hotel in Cusco for an evening meal.

Ron and Christine then visited the ruins of Machu Picchu, the lost city of the Incas the next day. Apart from a few locals, nobody knew of the city's existence until it was discovered by American historian Hiram Bingham on the 24th of July 1911. Today the city is the most visited archaeological site in Peru, but even with its influx of tourists, it manages to retain its air of grandeur and mystery. Ron and Christine visited the main plaza, the royal quarters, the temple of the three windows, the circular tower and the

Picchu Pueblo, before returning to their hotel in Cusco for the evening.

Ron and Christine spent the next day visiting Cusco's shops, doing a bit of sightseeing and visiting some of the local museums. In the evening they attended a traditional Peruvian dinner with a show at the La Ratama Peruvian restaurant, before returning to their hotel for the night.

They then boarded a train bound for Juliaca for their next trip. The eight-and-a-half-hour journey took them through the most spectacular landscapes which make up the Andean highlands, and through little traditional villages where they saw herds of limas and vicuñas. A first-class lunch was served on the train before they stopped at Puno, where they stayed at the Libertador Isla Esteves hotel for two nights.

The Libertador Isla Esteves hotel is situated on the shore of Lake Titicaca, the highest navigable lake in the world, three thousand eight hundred metres above sea level. After the next morning's breakfast, Ron and Christine went on a motor boat cruise on Lake Titicaca to visit the unique floating islands of the Uros. The tribe of people that inhabited the islands relied on the totter reed to build their floating villages and their modest homes and boats. Today only about three hundred people live on the islands, on which there are some schools and small museums.

After the morning cruise, Ron and Christine returned to the hotel for lunch. That afternoon they visited the chullpas of Sillustani, inhabited by the Colla people, who were originally a warlike tribe that dominated the Lake Titicaca area and later became a part of the Inca empire. Little is known about these people, but it is known that they buried their dead nobility in funeral towers complete with food and belongings for their journey into the next world.

After breakfast Ron and Christine were transported to Juliaca airport for the return two-and-a-half-hour flight to Lima. On landing they booked into the Jose Antonio Hotel for a three-night stay. The Jose Antonio Hotel is based in the Miraflores district of Lima, near the tourist and cultural

Machu Picchu the Lost City of the Incas

Libertador 5 Star Hotel Cusco Peru

The Condor Peru's National Symbol

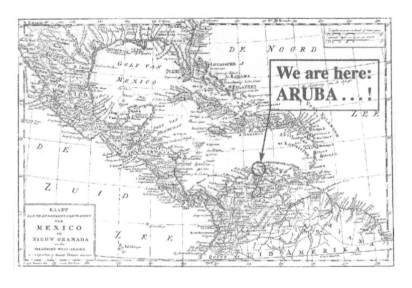

ARUBA "We are here...!" Map postcard

centres.

Ron and Christine enjoyed a morning's sightseeing tour of the city, with its legacy of art and architecture from its colonial period. Lima's museums are full of artefacts of gold, ceramics and weavings unearthed from the country's ancient settlements. The tour also included a visit to the gold museum in Lima. They returned to the hotel for a relaxing afternoon.

Shopping was the order of the next day. They visited Lima's boutiques and craft shops, full of gold and silver jewellery, leather, pottery, woven goods and wool-knitted items. Then they wandered around the plazas.

One of the highlights of Ron and Christine's visit was when they visited Ica to view the Nazca Lines. The Nazca Lines are a continuous unbroken line drawn in the fine dust of the ground, forming drawings of animals, which are viewed from the air. The nine thirty a.m. flight from Lima to Ica took one hour, and then Ron and Christine were flying over the Nazca Lines and seeing animals and geometric shapes, some of them over two hundred metres in length. It took over an hour to view one of the world's greatest sites.

The tour ended with a visit to Museum of Ica and the Huacachina Lagoon.

A special farewell dinner marked the end of Ron and Christine's visit to Peru. It was held at one of Lima's famous fish and seafood restaurants, La Rosa Nautica restaurant, located in a fabulous building at the end of a pier at Costa Verde in Miraflores.

The next morning they took a flight from Lima to Aruba in the Caribbean, spending a few days there relaxing, before flying back to Amsterdam and then on to Birmingham Airport and home.

Ron and Christine were then invited by friends to visit Kenya with them for Christmas in 2005. On arrival at Jomo Kenyatta International Airport, Ron and Christine booked into the Muthaiga Country Club for the night and had dinner at the Nairobi Hotel.

The Monkey and The Dog Nazca lines

A day at the races at Ngong Racecourse had been planned with a private box and lunch the next day, which was right up Ron and Christine's street. They then travelled to Naivasha to stay at the Oserian Wildlife Sanctuary at Chui Lodge on Lake Naivasha.

They spent a full day exploring the wildlife sanctuary, seeing the largest population of grey-crested helmet shrikes, other birds, leopards, buffalo, white rhinos, zebras and other animals roaming the sanctuary. The following day they explored the sanctuary further. Ron was offered the chance to ride or play polo at the end of the day, but Ron declined.

A boat ride on Lake Naivasha finalised their safari trip, and then they flew back to Malindi. There they stayed at a hotel close to the beach, but they had to evacuate in a hurry when they were caught in the middle of a tsunami. Ron remembers that the sea water was calm but was roaring when the tsunami struck. Luckily the rocks on the beach protected them, but in the port next to the beach boats were smashed to pieces and people lost their lives. Surviving a tsunami was one of the most amazing experiences of Ron's life, and it marked the end of their holiday.

In 2001 Ron and Christine arranged a trip to China. They boarded a plane at Birmingham Airport and flew to Frankfurt, Germany, then on to Shanghi Airport. They then booked into the Regal East Asia Hotel on arrival. That afternoon they visited the famous Yu Garden built during the Ming Dynasty and the Jade Buddha Temple before returning to the hotel for a meal then to bed.

A sightseeing tour of Shanghai city had been arranged, which included visits to the Nanjing road and the Shanghai Museum. The day finished with Ron and Christine seeing a performance by the amazing Shanghai acrobats.

On an excursion to Suzhou they visited the Humble Administrator's Garden, the largest of the city's many gardens, and the Lingering Garden. Then they took a forty-five-minute train ride through the countryside, seeing some of the rural life outside the city including farmers working in the paddy fields. The Suzhou area is also famous for its manufacturing of fine silk, so they visited the Silk Embroidery Institute and a silk factory before returning to the hotel in Shanghai.

They took an afternoon flight the next day to Yichang where they boarded the five-star *MS East Queen* cruiser. This was home for the next four nights as they cruised along the mighty Yangtze River. A variety of meals was made available, including Chinese and Western cuisines.

Motoring on up the Yangtze River, they saw the Three Gorges Dam, the largest project of its type in the world, due to be completed in 2009, which was 1,983 metres long and 185 metres high. In the afternoon they sailed through the Xiling Gorge, the largest of the three gorges around the dam. In the 1950s this would have been a very perilous journey by boat, before all the dangerous rocks in the river had been removed.

A Shennong Stream shore boat excursion was then taken. The stream joined the Yangtze River at Xirangkou. They continued their journey through the Wu Gorge, flanked by towering land peaks and mountains. They then passed through the Qutang Gorge, the shortest and the narrowest of the gorges.

The last visit on their boat trip the next day was to Shibaozhai pagoda, sometimes called the pearl on the Yangtze River, which is a building thirty metres wide and twelve storeys high built into the hillside on the banks of the river.

The day was completed with a farewell dinner on the *MS East Queen* hosted by the captain of the vessel. Then Ron and Christine disembarked at Chongqing and boarded a coach which took them to Dazu to see the rock carvings there. The fantastic display of Chinese grotto carvings illustrates almost every story in the Buddhist scripture with painstaking design and intricate, skilled chiselling. Next they flew to Xi'an where booked into the Garden Hotel.

One of the highlights of the next arranged tour was a visit

Ron and Christine's Chinese Boat Trip

Ron and Christine in a Chinese Rickshaw

The Chinese Terracotta Army

to the Terracotta Army. These life-sized infantry men, archers, chariots and horses symbolically guard the tomb of the first emperor of China, Qin Shi Huang, who for many years before his death conscripted thousands of the Chinese population to build a tomb and memorial as his resting place in his quest for the secret of immortality.

The purpose of the Terracotta Warriors was to protect the emperor in the afterlife, and to make sure that he had people to rule over in his next life. The Terracotta Army was only found by accident in 1974 at Xi'an. Local farmers digging a well broke into a pit containing six thousand terracotta figures. The site was then fully excavated in 1976 to reveal over eight thousand figures: warriors, chariots, horses, acrobats, strongmen and musicians.

The Terracotta Army figures were manufactured in workshops by government labourers and by local craftsman, with the heads, arms, legs and torsos being fired in the kilns and then assembled on a production-line type system. Upon completion, the figures were placed into the pits in precise military formation according to rank and duty. Originally, the figures were armed with real weapons such as spears, swords and crossbows, but it is thought that these were looted soon after the completion of the Terracotta Army.

After visiting the Terracotta Army, Ron and Christine finished the day with an arranged dumpling banquet and a Tang Dynasty music and dance show – a presentation of ancient music and dance from the Tang Dynasty, Its history dates back to local people performing a ritual for a good harvest or a better life. This developed into a new culture, introducing new musical instruments, singing and dancing with stunning costumes. The Xi'an Shaani provincial song and dance troupe inspired by China's thriving tourist industry conceived a series of programmes to illustrate on stage the history, culture and artistic heritage of Xi'an. This resulted in the Tang Dynasty music and dance show, being a regular tourist attraction, resulting in a great evening's entertainment for Ron and Christine.

The next morning Ron and Christine flew from Xi'an to Beijing to visit the Temple of Heaven. This complex of religious buildings was built as an altar of heaven, where the Chinese emperors came annually to pray for a good harvest. The Temple of Heaven is totally made out of wood, designed in a circle to represent heaven, and is thirty-six metres in diameter and thirty-eight metres tall. It is a major tourist attraction in Beijing.

Ron and Christine booked into the Guanghou Hotel in Beijing. In the evening they attended a performance of the Peking opera, which has a history of over two hundred years during which time it has influenced China's theatrical culture in many ways. It is a unique art form that combines acting, singing and music with martial arts and classical historical costumes.

Then Ron and Christine went sightseeing around Beijing visiting the Ming Tombs, a complex spreading over fifteen square miles in which sixteen Chinese emperors are buried along with their royal treasures. The entrance to the tombs is a great red gate where guards were originally posted to keep out the common people. The burial chambers are underground, with the typical imperial architecture surrounding the site painted in yellow, the favourite colour of emperors.

After this visit Ron and Christine went by coach to Badaling where they walked along the Great Wall of China, the single biggest tourist attraction in China. The Great Wall was originally built across the east-to-west line on the northern borders of China, to protect China from invasion by warlike forces between 220 and 206 BC.

The Great Wall was later a border control point, controlling trade routes into China and immigration and emigration in and out of the country.

The Great Wall's defences were further improved in later years by construction of watch towers with troops barracks. The top of the wall, five metres wide, acted as road for the transportation of goods.

Christine by the Yangtze River

The Great Wall of China dividing the country

The last day of Ron and Christine's trip to China they went to Tiananmen Square, the third largest public meeting place in the world and the centrepiece for several events in Chinese history. Then they moved on to the Forbidden City, so called because for over five hundred years only the emperor, his family and his entourage were allowed within its complex of courtyards, palaces and pavilions. Their last visit was to the Summer Palace, built on Longevity Hill alongside the manmade Kunming Lake, which covers 2.9 square kilometres. Longevity Hill is about sixty metres high and houses many buildings built in sequence. The front hill is covered with splendid halls and pavilions. In the lake in front of the Summer Palace is the marble boat, which sits in the water on a large stone-block base and is constructed from wood and painted to imitate a marble finish. It looks like an American paddle steamer but is a stationary object.

On returning to the hotel, they enjoyed a traditional Beijing duck banquet, which consisted of a duck roasted until the skin was crispy and then cut into one hundred and eight slices, served in pancakes with spring onions, cucumber and a sweet sauce.

At the end of Ron and Christine's visit to China. They caught a return flight from Beijing airport to Frankfurt and then to Birmingham and home.

Ron and Christine have been on several other holidays, including to Canada, where they visited Alaska, flying over the frozen lakes and seeing polar bears and seals in their natural environment, and the Rockies, travelling on the Rocky Mountain Railway. They also took a Norwegian cruise and visited the Canary Islands.

On a cruise to the Caribbean in 2012, a massive storm hit the ship, with waves coming over the bows over twelve metres high. When they reached Spain Ron took the decision to get off at the next port of call and fly back to England, as he did not feel safe on the boat. Ron and Christine still adventure abroad, and their next destination at the time of writing this book was Spain.

Epilogue

Ron has spoken about his next deal, but it seems likely that is now in his past. His is a life that has had its ups and downs, but he has enjoyed it to the full, working way past his official retirement age. He now has good memories of his achievements and the people he has met and worked with, and he would do it all again if he could live his life once more

At the time of writing this book Ron was ninety-six years of age and still going strong, with no regrets about the way life has turned out. Ron has had the most wonderful life, and has never done anybody a bad turn. Life's too short, he says.

Today Ron is settled with Christine in their cottage in Ditchling in Sussex and still has his interest in racing, whether watching the racing on the television or going to the races in Plumpton or Ascot to see his own horses hopefully winning.

Ron Muddle was at the start of this resurgence of horse-racing with his introduction of the all-weather racetrack, and he will always be remembered for changing the format of horse-racing for ever in England.

The Author and Ron Muddle

I am the son of Jack Kealey, who grew up with Ron in Jarvis Brook and kept in contact with him all his life. Ron was best man at Jack and Barbara's wedding, and Ron has known the author from the day he was born.

Ron used to visit Jack and his family when we lived in Hampshire. I remember as a kid Ron driving up in a Porsche 356 blue hard-top, which was when my interest in cars began. When myself and my brother Andrew were 15 and 14 years of age respectively, our family stayed with Vi at Buxford Farm for a holiday. In her Austin A55 Vi drove us all around Kent, sightseeing. We also had a trip on the *Carimuda* with Ron from Dover harbour, and myself and Andrew got involved in the haymaking, collecting the bales of straw from the fields with Johnny Holyer and Dave, who worked on the farm at Singleton Manor.

When Jack moved to Kent on his retirement and Ron converted the oast house flat for Jack and his family to live in, I transferred my coachbuilder's apprenticeship papers to be a motor mechanic and worked at County Motors, Ron's Ford main dealer, in Beaver Road, Ashford. Andrew worked at the Ashford railway works at Chart Leacon.

As the book shows, things changed at Singleton Manor, and I then went on the road for thirty years with an American corporation, demonstrating, selling and training mechanics in how to use engine diagnostic equipment. Andrew became a professional guitarist, moving to Nottingham. Ron kept in touch with the family.

I often visited Vi at Sandgate when I was on business in Folkestone, until Vi passed away at the age of one hundred and two.

It was on a visit to Ditchling that the idea for this book was emerged. I had spent the whole day with Ron and Christine, catching up with what had been happening in their lives, when Ron said, "I have got something to show you, boy." On entering a building outside Ron's cottage I found a full-sized snooker table covered in papers. Ron explained he was making notes for his biography, but had not got around to doing anything about it. I suggested that I could write up the papers that Ron had, if that was of any help, and try to make a biography from the information available. I then left Ron to think about it, and days later Ron called and said, "Well, when are you coming down to see me about writing up this biography?"

So, after several visits to Ron and his son, Richard, this book came about.

This book is not an in-depth biography, but it gives information on Ron's life, which I hope the reader finds of interest. Perhaps this book will give the reader the impetus to start their own business and travel the same road that Ron has in his life. What Ron created in the sport of kings was unique at the time and I hope that there are a few years left yet in this gentleman of horse-racing.

Ron, Mr Muddle and Peter at Ditchling 20-9-2012

Acknowledgements

First of all I would like to thank Ron and Christine for giving me the opportunity to write this, my first book, about an icon in the horse-racing world; for their help in obtaining the photographs and other information needed to complete this book; and for their hospitality on my visits to Ditchling for interviews with Ron.

Thank you to Richard Muddle, Jessica and family for their support, input and their hospitality on my visits, which included a trip to a polo match on Richard's polo field, a first for me.

Thank you to Nicola at Staples, Ashford, for helping me format the book binder for the book and the Staples staff, who are always happy to help their customers.

I would also like to thank the people who gave me permission to publish those photos in this book listed in the photo section, and Carly, for taking my author picture at Ditchling.

Thank you to Graham Bewley for formatting Ron's picture on the front cover of this book, and for checking the other photos in this book for the correct publishing DPI and colour matching (www.GrahamBewley.co.uk).

Thank you to Steve Baker of Ebooks by Design for converting my Word document into Kindle and Paperback formats; he did a great job (www.ebooksbydesign.co).

Thanks also to Derek Miller for allowing me to reproduce the information he obtained on the Buxted Muddles, in particular the information and photos of Thomas and Harriet, Ron's grandparents, and Albert and Vi Muddle, Ron's parents, from his Web site (www.MuddleFamilies.info).

I would also like thank Amazon for publishing this book. They have been very helpful in advising me on all the aspects of self-publishing, and I hope to produce more books through this channel in the future (www.amazon.co.uk).

And finally, thank you the purchaser of this book. I hope that you find Ron's story interesting for a read on the train or at home while relaxing. It is available on your Amazon Kindle, or in paperback for your bookshelf and for others to share in the future. If you would like to post your review and rate this book on the Amazon website for others to share your reading experience, please feel free.

Peter Kealey, author

Photos

1 Humble Beginnings

1	*Coopers Green Cottages*	*© Derek Miller*
2	*Thomas and Harriet Muddle*	*Private collection*
3	*Sopwith Camel F1*	*© Brooklands Museum Archive courtesy of BAE Systems*
4	*Bert and Vi*	*Private collection*
5	*Albert Muddle with Ron aged three*	*Private collection*
6	*Jarvis Brook Engineering*	*Private collection*
7	*The Muddles' caravan*	*Private collection*

2 The Spitfire Fuel Tank

8	*Spitfire fuel tank*	*© www.plane-design.com*
9	*Kenex Carefree caravan*	*Private collection*
10	*Southport Pier railway*	*© www.geraldengland.co.uk*
11	*Romney Hythe and Dymchurch railway*	*Private collection*

3 The Austin and Ford Dealerships

12	*Ron, Richard and Caroline at Singleton Manor*	*Private collection*
13	*Peacocks Ford dealer, Folkestone*	*Private collection*
14	*Richard and Caroline at Singleton*	*Private collection*
15	*Ford Anglia*	*©Malcolm Bishop www.spurrclassiccars.com*
16	*Ford Lotus Cortina MKI*	*© Malcolm Bishop www.spurrclassiccars.com*
17	*Ford MKII Zodiac*	*© Malcolm Bishop www.spurrclassiccars.com*

4 Ron's Life of Leisure and Sports

5 Ron's Other Businesses

6 Lingfield Park racecourse

7 Wolverhampton Racecourse

8 Retirement to the Country

9 World Travel

10 The Author and Ron Muddle

Index

China 97,101,104,
Coopers Green Cottages 3,4,
Commodore 47,
Concorde 61,
County Motors 31,33,
Cricket Matches 11,
Chris Buckley 25,26,
Crowborough 3,4,13,19,64,
Crowborough Football Club 8,
Cumbernauld 83,
Cyprus 67,71,

Dr Cyrus Poonawalla 85,
Dazu 98,
Delhi 89,90,
Derek Bretherton 57,
Dolphins 90,
Dover 12,19,20,21,22,39,51,55,107,

East German Republic 62,
Elephant 89,
Eric Oliver 35,
Equitrack 68,

Fairwarp 3,64,
Felixstowe Docks 57,
Folkestone Football Club 22,
Ford Dealership 31,33,
Ford Motor Company 27,31,
Ford Model T 8,
Fork Lift Driver 82,
Football 8,22,
Frank Sinatra 60,

Gatwick Airport 15,44,52,85,
Geneva 45,
George Parker 33,47,
Golf 22,33,37,38,60,63,68,76,81.82.
Goose 8,

Ham Polo Club 39,

Her Majesty Queen Elizabeth *11* 78,
HRH Princess Anne 76,
HRH Prince Charles 44,
HMS President *11* 4,
Hunter Trialling 39,
Hydraulic Steering Unit 52,

India 85,89,90,
Ionides Nelly 3,
Isle of Man TT 35,37,

Jockey Apprenticeship 67,
Jarvis Brook 4,7,8,28,107,
Jarvis Brook Engineering 4,15,
Jock (Stewart) 33,
Jockey Club 71,
John Dunlop 67,
Johnny Mulhern 40,
John Willment 63,
Jonah 49,50,
Junior School 12,

Kealey Jack 11,28,38,64,107,
Kealey Barbara 107,
Kealey Peter 107,
Kealey Andrew 107,
Kealey Billy (Grandfather) 3,11,
Kenex 12,21,
Kenya 95,

Lake Titicaca 92,
Leas Cliffe Hall 27,
Lester Piggott 60,83,
Lewes 3,
Libertador Hotel Cusco 91,
Lingfield Park Racecourse 68,71,73,
Las Vegas 61,
Lowestoft 51,
Lyng 7,
Lympne Airport 37,

Mac Wale 71,
Mahalakshmi Racecourse 85,
Manpower Board 20,
Manuel Ferreira 48,49,
Marbella Harbour 52,
Margey 13,
Mark Carrier 46,
Martins Garage 3,4,
Metal Aircraft Fuel Tanks 20,
Meux 55,
Miami 67,
Mid Sussex Golf Club 81,
Milk Marketing Board 62,
Motor Mechanic 3,4,13,
Muddle Albert (Bert) 3,
Muddle Caroline 28,39,46,47,63,
Muddle Christine 53,55,76,78,81,82,83,85,
Muddle Evelyn 13,14,
Muddle Harriet 3,
Muddle Joan 27,28,44,45,46,58,63,64,
Muddle Richard 28,39,46,47,64,67,71,77,81,
Muddle Ron 3,4,64,67,71,73,75,77,81,83,105,
Muddle Thomas 3,
Muddle Vi 4,8,12,13,14,15,19,64,71,73,

Nazca Lines 95,

Oserian Wildlife Sanctury 97,

Paul Withers 39,
Pembury Hospital 14,
Peru 91,95,
Peter Evans 60,
Peter Rowley 22,24,
Peter O'Sullevan 71,73,
Pfizer 25,26,
Plumpton Racecourse 81,82,83,
Polo 28,33,39,40,44,63,64,
Portobello Road 45,
Port of London Authority 21,
Portugal 48,49,50,57,

Pratts Petrol Cans 7,
Pre-fabricated Buildings 21,
Property Development 61,

Railway Works 31,107,
Richard Fenton 25,26,37,
Right Place at the Right Time 16,
Romney Hythe and Dymchurch Railway 21,
Royal Cinque Ports Golf Club 38,

Sally 16,19,21,
Sam Rocket 67,
Setabul Harbour 48,57,
Shell Mex Oil Company 7,12,
Singleton Manor 28,38,39,62,63,64,107,
Skiing 45,46,
Southampton Airport 14,
South Kent Technical College 31,
Southport Pier Railway 21,
Southwell Racecourse 53,75,77,81,
Suntester 31,
Squash 37,
Squeezebox 11,
Spitfire Fuel Tank 15,16,19,20,

Taiwan 53,
Taj Mahal 86,
Tang Dynasty 101,
Taxi 4,8,85,
Test Flights 14,15,
Tiananmen Square 104,
The Great Wall of China 102,
The Governor 20,
The Lost City of the Incas 91,
The Sport of Kings 108,
Tsunami 97,

Uckfield Grammer School 12,

Vendome 4,
Vickers Spitfire Assembly Plant 14,

Wheeler and Dealer 82,
Wilf Amory 22,24,
Wolverhampton Racecourse 77,78,81,
Woodrow Wyatt 77,
World Cup Final 1966 24,

X Ray 63,
Xian 98,101,

Yangtze River 98,

Printed in Great Britain
by Amazon

78515102R00078

G000162800

THE DOG LOVER'S A TO Z

THE DOG
LOVER'S
A TO Z

Clare Faulkner

quadrille

INTRODUCTION

If you are reading this book, you are highly likely to be a cynophile –
but check out the Cs if you are in any doubt! I hope you will enjoy
weaving through this A to Z of all things canine and sharing in the joy
our furry pals bring us. While this book is intended as a light-hearted
guide, I do hope it provides some helpful advice along the way. You
could dip in and out or read it from A to Z, it is entirely up to you,
but ideally do it with a dog curled up beside you.

Dogs and humans have a long and unique relationship going back
thousands of years, but our bond is constantly evolving. In recent
years, many people have taken the plunge and become devoted dog
parents and our parks and streets are packed with a dazzling range
of distinctive breeds and characterful mutts. There is no doubt we
love our dogs and most of us now consider our pets a bone-fide
member of the family. Indeed, many people and their beloved pets
are enjoying the physical and mental health benefits that this special
relationship provides. However, along with this increase in dog
ownership has come some inevitable problems, so be sure to do
plenty of research before you welcome a new dog into your life.

Any dog paw-rent will tell you, no matter the size or breed, the commitment is fur real and, as a dog lover, a healthy and happy doggo will be number one on your list. Of course, different breeds can seem a world apart, and we all have our fur-avourites that somehow set our hearts aflutter (Whippets, Samoyeds and Shiba Inus in our own paw-ticular case). Understandably, many people find the looks of certain breeds difficult to resist, but hard as it might be to accept, they may not be the woofer for you and your situation. If you find the right match for your lifestyle, you will both reap the rewards, and you can look forward to a priceless bond that will bring you joy, soothe you after a hard day and make you laugh like never before, but always be prepared for the ruff along with the smooth, as no dog is paw-fect and nor should we expect them to be!

See ADOPTION, CROSSBREED, CYNOPHILE, IDIOCY, JAPANESE SHIBA INU, JOY, PEDIGREE, SAMOYED, WHIPPET

Dream dogs: the soulful Whippet and the floofy Samoyed

Your doggo will humbly thank you for keeping accessories to a minimum

ACCESSORIES

There is a wondrous world of shopping out there for your pooches, from dapper bowties and jewel-encrusted collars to Halloween outfits and matching hoodies for doggo and owner. There is plenty to tempt you to part with your hard-earned cash but let's remember that just because you can, doesn't mean you should. Some dogs are happy to go along with the fun, but make sure they are not uncomfortable or in danger of getting hot under the collar in more ways than one. *See also* COATS. COLLARS

ADOPTION

There are many dogs needing homes, and maybe your perfect match is waiting paw-tiently to join you. If you have a specific breed in mind, you may find one in a shelter, or they are often rehomed by breed associations. You may be able to skip the crazy puppy phase and adopt an older pooch, but there are also sometimes puppies needing homes. With an older dog, you should be able to get a good idea of their behaviour and needs, and rehoming centres will take the time to make sure you are a good fit. #adoptdontshop *See also* RESCUE. UNDERDOG

AFFECTION

From those soft, soulful stares to the gentlest nuzzles, through (sometimes not so welcome) face licks and the cutest tentative lean-ins, our best pals have many ways to express their abundant affection for us. Your dog will greet you in the way, let's face it, a human rarely does – with unfailing enthusiasm and child-like excitement. Dogs' affection knows no bounds and is guaranteed to soothe you after a ruff day. This emotional bonding with your pooch is also im-paw-tant for your dog, and your affection in return will make your dog feel safe and secure. *See also* ENTHUSIASM, LOVE, OXYTOCIN, STARING, WAGGING

AFGHAN HOUND

These eye-catching hounds are famous the world over for their luscious silky locks and sophisticated elegance. While they give off an air of snootiness, they are known for their giddy moments that will charm the socks off you. Unsurprisingly, these floofy athletes need copious amounts of grooming and exercise. *See also* FLOOFBALL

The Afghan Hound is proud to be the poshest dog on the block

AGEING

Our beloved doggos will gradually slip into canine retirement with varying degrees of dignity, and you might observe an increase in gassiness and slobber as well as those predictable expanding waistlines and emerging health troubles. However, your senior mutt is likely to be more laid-back than they were in their youth, and you can look forward to more time putting your feet up together. Sadly, older dogs are often overlooked for adoption, but they can make incredibly loyal and rewarding companions. *See also* ADOPTION, CHONK, LOYALTY

AGGRESSION

It's one thing to have a toy pooch baring their teeth at you, and quite another to be faced with a snarling great woofer, but all dogs are capable of this natural canine behaviour. Aggression includes a whole range of actions, from growling and teeth-baring to air biting and real biting. It is a normal expression of emotion and a coping behaviour that is usually associated with fear. A dog may use a series of non-aggressive signals to express stress or discomfort before escalating to aggressive actions and it's vital for dog paw-rents to learn to read them. Dogs will rarely go for full aggression without giving warning signs, so look out for freezing, flirting (attempting to de-escalate a situation) and flight. Aggression is one of the most common behavioural problems that owners seek help for and a reason many dogs end up in shelters, so if you spot non-aggressive signs of fear, try to figure out the cause and deal with it before they escalate into aggression when you could need to get the help of a professional behaviourist. *See also* ANGER, BITING, GROWLING

AGILITY

Agility training classes and competitions are great fun for owners and dogs alike and will have the added bone-us of keeping you both in tip-top shape. Stars of the agility scene include the Border Collie, Poodle and Cocker Spaniel but mixed breeds can often excel too.

AIREDALE TERRIER

Often declared the 'King of the Terriers', perhaps for their characterful and handsome looks and their comparatively large size, these clever and determined dogs will need plenty of exercise and entertainment and love nothing more than a challenging activity.

An enthusiastic star of the agility scene

ALLERGY

Unfortunately, some dog lovers encounter a catalogue of troublesome allergy symptoms from sneezing and wheezing to coughing and rashes, most often caused by dander flying around the home. Of course, speak to your doctor for advice if you suspect you have an allergy to your dog, but there are things you can do at home to try to reduce the impact. We know they won't be impressed, but you may have to keep them out of the bedroom and ideally off soft furnishings too. Wash their bedding often on a hot wash and consider investing in an air purifier. Military-style house cleaning and regularly grooming and washing your dog will help too. *See also* CROSSBREED, FUR

ANGER

Like us, dogs experience a range of emotions and though it can be unsettling to think our doggos feel some of the more unpleasant emotions, correctly reading their body language is vital for paw-sitive dog-human interactions. Anger is probably a rarer emotion for our pets than irritation or fear but learning to read the warning signs can stop escalation in its tracks. A study showed that dogs can also tell the difference between a happy and an angry human face and are very skilled at reading our expressions, so try as you mutt, you can't hide your anger from your pup.
See also AGGRESSION. MOODS

ANTHROPOMORPHISM

It's cute to believe our pups have the same understanding of the world we do, and it is fun to imagine our doggies feeling bad for their misdeeds and there is no doubt they can look pretty guilty at times! However, many behavioural problems can stem from our high expectations of our pets by attributing complex human emotions to them, and it can hinder our relationships and human-dog bond. Let our dogs be dogs. See also DOG SHAMING. MISCHIEF. NO. STUBBORNNESS

ANXIETY

Our doggos are efficient communicators and will use a whole range of signs to tell us they are feeling nervy or anxious, but whether we pick up on them is another matter. From clues such as lip licking, sidling away and pinned back ears, to the more glaringly obvious such as cowering, whale eye or a tail tucked between their legs, there are many indicators of a worried best fur-iend. Don't force your dog to do things that are out of their comfort zone but try to work on building their confidence with patience, careful training and help from a behaviourist. One of the most common forms of anxiety is separation-related and many dogs find it hard to be left alone, even if they don't show any obvious signs. It helps to gradually increase the time they are left, starting with just leaving the room, and when you are going out try to reduce external noise, have a walk before, leave an entertaining chew toy or favourite comforter and make use of dog sitters or walkers.

See also BLANKETS, CHEWING, DOG SITTERS, DOG WALKERS, FIREWORKS, HOWLING, LOUD NOISES, ROUTINE, WHALE EYE

*Awooing for
some attention*

THE DOG LOVER'S A TO Z

ATTENTION

From bringing us random gifts and dry humping to plaintively sighing and making mischief, our doggos are experts at getting our attention and it can be easy to reinforce this without really meaning to! It takes some restraint but try to reward them with your attention when they are doing the right thing instead. Excessive or bothersome attention-seeking could be caused by boredom or not getting enough exercise, as some dogs need lots of mental and physical stimulation, so try to up the entertainment in their life. *See also* CHEWING, HUMPING, MISCHIEF, SIGHING, WFH

AUSTRALIAN SHEPHERD

The 'Aussie' is bizarrely not, in fact, from Australia but is thought to have originated in the Pyrenees. These beautiful dogs with impressive coats are very clever and are often working dogs, so they will need lots of brain workouts, attention and exercise. If these doggos don't get enough mental and physical stimulation, that energy will be channelled into mischief.

AWOO

Another word for a good old howl. *See also* BARK

The well-floofed Aussie

BALLS

From the classic tennis ball to the football or even enormous inflatables, most dogs love a ball – and a drool-covered ball deposited at your feet, or if you're really lucky, in your lap, is a sure sign your dog loves a game of fetch. Have a warm-up first and you could try other bonding games, like tug-of-war or a treat hunt, when you're out walking, if your pet is a little too crazy for balls. Avoid much-loved tennis balls becoming chew toys as they can wear down precious teeth when fine grit builds up on them. Ap-paw-rently blue and yellow balls are the easiest colours for your canine to spot. *See also* STICKS, TOYS, TUG-OF-WAR

BARK

Their bark is worse than their bite may not always be the case, though it must be said barking can sometimes be a right pain. Fascinatingly, although barking is used frequently by our furry pals, it is rarely used in the wild. Barking is a natural method of communication which can mean your dog is worried, bored or wants attention. Try to work out the reason for disruptive barking, then increase their exercise and play if that's what they need. Try not to reward persistent barking; instead ignore them and avoid eye contact until they stop, then give a reward.

BARKITECTURE

From in-built canine wash stations in the laundry, to cosy sleeping nooks under the stairs and even fully furnished mini apartments, the internet is awash with doggy house design. Your dog is unlikely to care whether they bathe in the human bath or a bespoke doggy shower room, but it seems there is something deeply satisfying about the world of barkitecture for many dog fans. #barkitecture

BASSET HOUND

These charming characters are famous for their doleful looks, which contrast with their friendly natures. Their impressively long, flapping ears and unusual wrinkles need some extra care. You might need to keep an eye on their waistlines, as they are known for their enthusiasm at mealtimes, and they'll do wonders for your biceps as you hoist them into the car.

BATHS

Some dogs love a bath, while others dread the experience, but most will learn to stoically suffer their fate. Luckily most dogs don't need bathing very often, it depends greatly on the breed, but it's inevitable that your dog will occasionally get itself into a mess, whether it's a joyful roll in some fox poo or a spectacularly muddy puddle. You can avoid too much chaos at home if you prepare well before your dog realizes what is coming. You'll need a suitably sized bath or container for smaller pooches, special dog shampoo, a non-slip mat if you're using your bath, towels, and treats at hand. Be ready for the inevitable dramatic shake, all over you, of course, at the end. Dogs also love a roll around after their baths to try to regain that lovely fur-miliar doggy smell. *See also* FOXES, GROOMING, POOP, UNSAVOURY SMELLS, WASHING

A Lurcher stoically accepting their fate

BEAGLE

These fetching dogs are famous for their endearingly sweet faces and agreeable natures, but are reportedly a little on the mischievous side and don't like to be left alone. They love their food, so watch out for budding chonks, and they will need lots of exercise to wear them out. Beagles make a distinctive baying sound shared with other scent hounds, which is sure to raise a few eyebrows.

The fur-iendly Beagle

BEARD

There is something distinguished about a dog with an impressive beard and some breeds to consider if you are after a pooch with characterful facial hair include Schnauzers, Airedale Terriers, Bearded Collies and Irish Wolfhounds. While there is no doubt they look charming, those beards are also likely to get mucky, and may need some extra grooming. *See also* FLOOFBALL, GROOMING

BEDS

It can be hard to know what to choose for your furry friend, when there is such a variety of beds available to spend your hard-earned cash on. Observe any dog and they are likely to have an impressive range of sleeping positions that need to be catered for. Round beds are snug and cosy for curling up in, but your pooch may want to stretch out sometimes, so an alternative sleeping place might be needed too. But ultimately, it's im-paw-tant your dog can snuggle down in peace and quiet when it chooses and get some undisturbed shut eye. Whatever bed you and your dog choose, you can bet they'll spend some quality time faffing around getting everything just right before a snooze. They will probably pre-fur your bed, of course, as it smells so comfortingly of you. *See also* BASKETS, BEDTIME, BLANKETS, NAP, SLEEP

BEDTIME

Just like with children, bedtime for our fluffy pals can be a fraught time in some households. Some dogs will get anxious as the evening draws to an end, others will get the zoomies, but a well-established bedtime routine will let your dog know what to expect and soothe those nerves. Give your dog some top-notch attention in the run-up to bedtime, and make sure they are tired out and have been to the toilet. Whether your dog sleeps in your bedroom, in the kitchen or elsewhere, a safe and cosy space is essential. Puppies will need lots of support while they get used to a routine and will need to sleep near you initially. Any new puppy owner will tell you it's like having a human baby and you need to be prepared for some ruff days ahead! *See also* BEDS, FRAP, SLEEP, ZOOMIES

BELLY RUBS

One of life's great pleasures is indulging in a joyful belly rub with a human's best friend. Rolling around on the floor in doggy bliss while you stroke that most vulnerable of areas, bonds you with your pooch in a unique way and benefits you both. However, not all dogs love a belly rub and that's okay – they might pre-fur pleasing chin rubs or affectionate head scratches. Also watch their signals, if a dog is avoiding eye contact and looks tense, they may be nervous and displaying submission rather than requesting a belly rub. *See also* CUDDLES, EARS

BICHON FRISE

These dogs are the ultimate balls of floof and can be trimmed, much like the Poodle, into pleasing shapes. A fair amount of grooming will be required for these playful little bundles of joy but on the plus side, they don't shed much and if you like your dogs very cute, this could be the pooch for you. *See also* FLOOFBALL

BIRDS

Many of us are aware of the havoc cats can cause on the bird population, but unfortunately our beloved dogs can also have a big impact on our wild birds too, in ways that may not be immediately obvious, such as disturbing ground-nesting birds when they approach. Making sure your dog-walking follows the regulations in the countryside, such as adhering to short-lead rules during nesting season, can make a huge difference to birds' survival. Chasing is also, of course, a normal impulse for dogs, and some with higher prey drives will benefit from toys and games that allow them to safely indulge this instinct and hopefully leave the birds in peace. *See also* PREY, TOYS

BITCH

In this A to Z, it means a female pooch and we'll leave it there. *See also* HEAT, STUD

BITING

Ouch! Puppies love to bite – it is, after all, a natural instinct for all dogs but it can be pretty challenging (and painful) at times to deal with. Just like human babies, dogs want to put everything in their mouths to discover the world and that includes you! You should ignore a puppy biting and redirect it to something it can safely bite instead, such as a chew toy. Your pup needs to learn good chewing habits and not to chew on you. A basic training course will help you to control your dog's behaviour alongside socializing and building confidence. Remember that all dogs can bite, so look out for signs in their body language or vocalizations that indicate they are afraid or stressed, so you can deal with the situation before they bite. See also AGGRESSION, CHEWING, JAWS

BLANKETS

Many dogs will have a special blanket that makes them feel safe, is cosy to get wrapped up in and is likely to reduce their anxiety. Their blanket smells familiar and, of course, of you, and whether your dog drags their favourite one around with them, or churns it around in their bed, there is likely to be a good deal of faffing with the soft fluffy stuff from your doggo. See also ANXIETY, BEDS, BEDTIME, NAPS, SLEEP

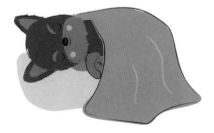

A fur-avourite blanket moment

THE DOG LOVER'S A TO Z

BLOODHOUND

These droopy-faced sleuths have an impressive sense of smell and have a long history of tracking criminals and assisting with searches. Although gentle in nature, they are not a dog for the novice and their physical and health needs should be researched.

BLOP

An endearing moment when your furry friend forgets to put their tongue completely away. #blop See also LICKING, MLEM, TONGUE OUT TUESDAY

BONES

Although dogs love a good old chew on a bone and it gives them a great deal of pleasure, splintering is a very real danger and small bones, such as chicken or chops, or cooked bones are definite no-nos. It's a surprisingly controversial issue and you should consult your vet about whether to feed your dog raw bones; if you do, make sure you supervise them. There are plenty of tasty alternative chews out there. See also CHEWING, TREATS

Be sure to bone up on safe chews for your pup

BOOP

The gentlest little affectionate nudge from your doggo, especially a wet nose boop or a pat with their paw. Of course, it's hard to resist a little tap with our finger on their cute noses too. #boop See also AFFECTION, NOSES, NUZZLE, PEETS

BORDER COLLIE

These supremely clever canines need plentiful exercise and mental stimulation to keep them busy and out of mischief. Brimming with energy, they are popular su-paw-stars on the agility circuit and are highly trainable. As classic as they come. *See also* BRAINS

The Border Collie is always up fur a challenge

BORDER TERRIER

Healthy, friendly and intelligent balls of fun, Border Terriers have lots of energy to expend. Their strong characters and cheeky-faced looks make them one of the most popular terriers.

BOXER

Ap-paw-rently these over-sized puppies love a fuss and have big personalities to match their mighty chests. They will devotedly guard their humans and are loved family pets but don't like being on their own and are prone to some health troubles.

BRAINS

Whether you have a goofball or a superbrain at home, many of us have boasted of our pooch's intellectual prowess. There is no denying dogs have excelled in managing us humans and some of the breeds generally thought of as highly intelligent, such as Border Collies, have learnt extraordinary skills and responsiveness. But interestingly dogs are not as good problem solvers as some other clever animals. One study revealed some individual dogs have exceptional intelligence, and whether your furry friend at home is one of those or not is not really the point, as we tend to favour affection at home.

*If only brushing was
always this simple*

BRUSH

Whether you have a pooch that requires daily grooming, like the labour-intensive Poodle, or a short-haired mutt that needs only an occasional brush down, it can be hard to know how to choose the paw-fect brush for your beloved doggo. Double-sided brushes are a good go-to option, with pins on one side for detangling and bristles on the other for smoothing and floofing. Show your dog their brush for a good sniff and to get their approval before you begin. *See also* ALLERGY, COATS, FUR, GROOMING

BULLDOG

Their unmistakeable looks have made them famous the world over, but today's Bulldogs belie their imposing appearance with gentle, though a little stubborn, natures. Walking takes a little more effort for these stocky characters, so take their lead and find an exercise routine that suits you both. They are sadly prone to a plethora of health problems, which can be expensive and hard for your pup and you, so do your research before choosing this breed.

BULL TERRIER

These powerful, solid dogs have distinctive oval shaped heads, dark eyes and curious pointed ears. Bullys are said to be very active and great fun but would only suit an experienced owner.
See also TERRIERS

CANINE

Dog or dog-like. The long pointy canine tooth is named after dogs, who, of course, have much more impressive ones than we do. Often K9 too, which is also the nickname for police dogs. *See also* TEETH

CARRIERS

Maybe you have a little fur baby, or your dog is getting older and finding long walks a challenge and it is time to invest in a cosy carrier to give them a rest or keep them safe in busy areas. There are plenty to choose from, depending on the size and weight of your pooch, from pillowy soft bags to adorable backpacks and slings. It is true there is little cuter than a dog poking its head out of a bag but make sure you have one that is a comfortable fit for your four-legged friend. They should be able to easily pop their head out or it should have good ventilation and don't over-do it, or they could overheat or get uncomfortable in there. Of course, if you're travelling on a plane, you'll need to make sure your carrier fits the regulations and is safe for travel.

CATS

The internet is awash with dogs and cats who are fur-ever friends – adorably snoozing, playing and grooming together – but unfortunately this is not always the case. While it is very possible for dogs and cats to live in domestic bliss, some are better matches than others. For the pups with a high prey drive, there is nothing more tempting than chasing a passing kitty and this can be hard to suppress, while cats of a more sensitive nature may find all dogs too boisterous. If you want to have both fur babies in your life, it helps if you introduce them when they are little, but this is not always paws-ible, so a slow, cautious introduction is recommended, starting with their scent.

CAVALIER KING CHARLES SPANIEL

These popular miniature spaniels have long silky fur, which will need a fair amount of grooming, and super cute faces. They are masters of the puppy dog eyes and will charm the socks off their families. This breed is said to be very friendly but won't appreciate being left on their own. *See also* KING CHARLES SPANIEL

CHEWING

Chewing is a natural and normal instinct for our pooches, but unfortunately it can drive us up the wall when they make a beeline for our possessions. Puppies and teens have a manic need to chew to soothe teething gums but all dogs will enjoy a good chomp to exercise their jaws, keep their teeth clean and relieve anxiety or perhaps brighten a dull day. If your dog is infuriating you by munching your belongings, try to keep them safely out of reach, but be quick to replace them with an item they can chew safely and be sure to make a big fuss when they do chew the right things. Chewing can also be a great stress reliever, so a long-lasting chew to munch on can be helpful in some situations. *See also* ANXIETY, ATTENTION, BITING, JAWS, SHOES, TEETH

CHIHUAHUA

Pocket-sized pooches with fire in their tummies, these popular pups have big personalities housed within their tiny frames. They come with soft, smooth coats or long, flowing ones and be sure to watch out for them under your clumsy human feet. *See also* SMOL, TOY DOGS

Do not underestimate the mighty Chihuahua!

CHOCOLATE

Be sure to keep your precious chocolate stash out of paws reach, because, rather cruelly, chocolate is toxic to dogs. Unfortunately, some dogs, just like us, find the allure of chocolate too hard to resist and if you think your pup has eaten some, speak to your vet immediately. Holiday seasons can be particularly fraught with danger and there is a handy online chocolate calculator to consult for toxicity guidance if you know how much your pup has consumed. *See also* TOXIC

CHONK

An affectionate name for the more rotund pooch. If you suspect you have a chonk on your hands, you may need to take a long hard look at their diet and lifestyle to get them back to tip-top shape. You might think they look cute, and indeed they do, but you're doing the health of your furry friend no favours. A trip to the vet will help you tackle even the heftiest of weights and you can look forward to a sprightly new pup. *See also* DIETS

A chonky boy

CHOPS

Another word for jowls, this is a word often wheeled out in the huge array of nicknames you give your doggo. Maybe you have a messy chops or perhaps a sloppy chops in your household? *See also* JOWLS

CHOW CHOW

Although these chunky doggos look like enormous cuddly bears, they are re-paw-ted to be a little aloof and may not appreciate being lavished with affection, so may not be the best choice for a family dog. Those impressive manes and puffy chests that give them the distinctive floofball appearance can leave them vulnerable to overheating, and they are prone to a few health issues, so do find a responsible breeder and investigate their needs before choosing a Chow Chow. *See also* FLOOFER

CHUFFING

Also known as huffing. *See also* BARK, COMMUNICATION, HUFFING

CLAWS

Luckily most dogs don't need to have their claws trimmed very often and some won't need to at all. Claws are naturally filed by walking on hard surfaces but whether your dog needs their claws clipped will depend on their breed, exercise levels, the surfaces they walk on, and their weight. Dog claws are blunter than a cat's because they are always out and get smoothed down walking around. Dewclaws are a little higher up and might require some more care because they don't make as much contact with the ground. It can save you a lot of stress further down the line if you get your pup used to having their paws handled from an early age. *See also* PADS, PAWS, PEETS

Looking dapper in the paw-fect coat

COATS

Although our furry friends obviously come with their own beautiful coats, some of our pooches may need a little extra help in the winter months. Of course, some dogs, like the Siberian Husky, are built for the cold with their thick fur, while others, such as the tiny Chihuahua, are going to be shivering very quickly in the cold. While it might be tempting to choose the cutest clothing going, it's most im-paw-tant to get a good snug fit for your pup, but not too tight, so they can go about their usual business comfortably. Their coat should do the job of keeping them warm and dry and if it happens to look smart too, that's a bone-us!

COBBY

Short and solid, but compact doggos, like a Pug. We're not saying chonk, but... *See also* CHONK

COCKAPOO

An endearing crossbreed of the Cocker Spaniel and the Poodle. These cuddly bears are said to be friendly and lovable and are a popular choice for families, but they are an energetic and intelligent mix so will need plenty of attention and stimulation to keep them content. Grooming needs will vary depending on whether your pup ends up with more of the Cocker or the Poo to their coats. *See also* COCKER SPANIEL, POODLE

Often mistaken for a teddy bear, the Cockapoo

COCKER SPANIEL

The English Cocker Spaniel has long, characterful ears and soulful eyes to melt your heart. Originally bred to flush out woodcocks, they are busy little bees and like to be involved in everything you do. The American Cocker Spaniel has much longer silky locks.

COLLARS

From classic leather to on-trend designs with matching bowties through sparkly jewel-encrusted dazzlers, there is a dumbfounding range of collars available to suit every furry pal out there. Although looking dapper is likely to be high on your list, ensure you find a comfortable and safe collar for your pooch. Spending a little more, especially for a grown-up dog, is likely to pay off for quality and longevity. In the UK, all dogs must wear a collar with an ID tag in a public place, even if they are microchipped, and an ID tag is also required in the US. Hands up who thinks their dog looks naked without their collar?

COMMUNICATION

Our pooches are remarkably adept at understanding us, which is not that surprising when you appreciate we have specifically selected and bred dogs for their superior social skills. A study suggested dogs are more patient with us when we accidentally drop a treat than if we withhold it, revealing a sophisticated understanding of our intentions. Dogs also use scent, sound and body language to communicate with each other. Another study using software to identify barks in different contexts, has suggested dogs have certain barks that can be universally understood by each other. AI could in time be used by humans to help understand their pet dogs and translate those nuanced sounds for us, which could be beneficial for dogs with behavioural problems and potentially save some from the shelter.

Taking the time to try to understand your pup's signals better will hugely improve both your relationship and their behaviour.
See also BARKS, HOWLING, HUFFING, TAILS

CONE OF SHAME

This undignified milestone in every dog's life is one everyone is sure to remember. Whether your dog has been injured, spayed or neutered, the ungainly Elizabethan-style collar will surely come out at some point to prevent them interfering with their wounds. It's a miserable experience for the whole household while your poor dog navigates their newly restricted life with a lampshade on their head. They will use all the body language at their disposal to communicate their displeasure and pull at your heart strings – but stay strong! There are some new alternatives to consider, so talk to your vet if your dog is completely wretched.
See also NEUTERING

The cone of shame, an undignified milestone

CORKSCREW

If the iconic corkscrew perm of the Eighties is your thing, you might want to consider a Bichon Frise or Pumi, two breeds with the big hair you crave. *See also* BICHON FRISE, GROOMING

COURTSHIP

Many male pups reach sexual maturity as early as six months and they are ready for action at any time and not that fussy about who they court. A male can pick up on a fertile female's scent in her urine from long distances. A bit like humans, different dogs behave in varying ways; some will act as if they aren't that bothered while others will find it hard to hide their enthusiasm! The male will have a good sniff at her rear and if she's ready, she may move her tail to the side, a clear sign she's keen. *See also* BITCH, HUMPING, STUD

CRATES

Who doesn't want their own cosy den to retreat to for some 'me' time now and then? These indoor kennels come in all sorts of designs and materials, but the most popular are those with wire frames. Your fur-avourite canine's sanctum should be big enough for them to easily sit up, turn around, stretch and lie down. You can cover the top and sides with a sheet to make it feel extra snug and there should be comfy bedding, water and a chew toy. This should be a safe place for your pup and not used as a reprimand, and be sure to only leave them in their den for short periods. If your dog goes in of their own accord, they should be left in peace in their safe space.
See also BEDS

CRONCH

Crunching in dog speak, something a dog just loves to do. #cronch *See also* CHEWING

*Cronching on
a carrot*

The Jug, a Jack Russell crossed with a Pug

CROSSBREED

From Schnoodles and Dorgis to Jugs and Jackabees, the adorable names are without doubt very cute, but the recent popularity of crossbreeds, which mix two or more breeds, has led to some genuine concern about the rise of so-called 'designer dogs'. Often thought to be perfect family pets, sometimes the high expectations aren't matched by the reality. The significant prices they demand has led to some unscrupulous breeders exploiting the market, so make sure you carefully research your breeder, always see your pup more than once before bringing them home and ensure you see them with Mum. If you are ever unsure, chat to your vet or look for the 'puppy contract' online for some guidance. *See also* COCKAPOO, LABRADOODLE

CUDDLES

Yes, we want our dogs to be our teddy bears, but while some are cuddle bugs, many simply find it too much. Look out for their body language when going in for a hug to make sure they are happy with the situation. Clues they are finding your affections stressful include going very still, showing the whites of their eyes, yawning or shaking it off. If you stop mid-hug and create a little distance, does your dog come in for more hugs or are they pleased the cuddle is over? *See also* OXYTOCIN

CYNOPHILE

That's likely to be you: a dog lover!
#doglover #lovemydog #ilovedogs #dogsarefamily #doggylove

The famous Doxie

DACHSHUND

These comedic little
dogs, distinctive for
their long, thin bodies
and short legs, just
love to dig. They need
a reasonable amount of
exercise and play to stave off their chonky tendencies. Affectionately
known as Sausage Dogs and Doxies, they come in various varieties,
such as smooth-haired and wire-haired. Some are prone to back
problems, so be sure to choose a responsible breeder and be aware
some insurance policies may exclude spine-related issues. Re-paw-ts
suggest they can be a little on the stubborn side.

DALMATIAN

Famous the world over for their un-fur-gettable black or dark brown
spots, these leggy dogs are sure to get some admiring looks when
out on the town. However, they demand lots of exercise, so make
sure you research their high energy needs before welcoming one
through your door and they will need patient and consistent training
to influence their big personalities.

DELIVERIES

Spare a thought for the trembling couriers and posties out there
who risk life and limb, encountering dogs that really don't appreciate
their im-paw-tant work. If your pup likes to rip your post to shreds,
consider a wire letter box or an outside mailbox, then you can safely
retrieve your mail when the dog is having a snooze.

A derpy moment

DERP

When you catch your giddy pup being a bit of a derp, they are likely to have their tongue hanging out, or their eyes crossed, or they're having one of those special zoomie moments reserved for only the silliest of dogs. #derp *See also* BLOP, FRAP, IDIOCY, INSANITY

DETECTION

Our amazing super-sleuths are doing extraordinary work around the world assisting humans in all sorts of ways. As well as tracking down criminals, finding drugs and explosives, sniffer dogs are helping make strides in medicine by detecting many diseases including malaria, bladder cancer, covid and Parkinson's. Impressively, they are also being used to help in conservation, putting their miraculous snuffly noses to work tracking down a variety of endangered and rare species including great nested newts, pine martens and dormice. *See also* BLOODHOUND

Detective Dawg

DEVOTION

Let's face it, the kind of devotion a dog offers you is rarely found anywhere else. It's fantastic for your ego to have that goofy face gazing adoringly at you, over the moon to have you home at last. Who else follows you around, excited just to be in your sublime presence? *See also* AFFECTION, ENTHUSIASM, LOVE

DIETS

Dogs are natural scavengers and it is instinctive for them to snaffle anything tasty that comes their way. They are also incredibly adept at giving you those puppy dog eyes whenever your own food comes out, but unfortunately too many treats can lead to a chonky pup. While a chubby dog can indeed look cute, the fun soon stops when your beloved doggo suffers health problems or has a shortened life unnecessarily. It won't be easy, but planning with your vet will quickly help your well-rounded dog get back in shape. You will need nerves of steel to resist those pitiful looks and you must doggedly stick to the regime! *See also* CHONK, FOOD, TREATS

DIGGING

Some dogs just love to dig and there are breeds that are naturally programmed to get down in the dirt. Terriers, Dachshunds and Beagles have been bred to dig and it can be hard for them to resist this impulse. If your dog is busy making Swiss cheese of your garden, you might want to consider fencing a small area or filling a sandpit with soil for your pet, where they are able to indulge in their favourite pastime without tearing up your plants while you tear your hair out.
See also GARDENS

DISCIPLINE

As a dog lover, you will want to focus on paw-sitive reinforcement rather than punishment. Dogs often don't understand why they are being punished and fail to associate their behaviour with the penalty.

Digging up trouble

Although our doggos can frustrate us with their antics, disciplining them with harsh words, or worse, can break our special bond and make behaviour deteriorate further. *See also* TRAINING

DOBERMANN

The ultimate guard dog, handsome and powerful, so needing plenty of exercise and stimulation. Its affectionate and loyal nature make it a popular family dog, although its loyalty may be to one member, in particular. Despite their striking looks that intimidate some, Dobies are reported to be well-behaved and faithful if given the right training. *See also* GUARDING

DOG DAD/MUM

Human paw-rent to a canine fur baby. Just like any parent, a Dog Dad or Mum must guide their furry charge through life's ruff and tumble. A rewarding but demanding job any cynophile is happy to undertake. *See also* CYNOPHILE, FUR BABY

DOG SHAMING

If you have caught your pup in the act of something shameful, you can disgrace them on the internet alongside a crudely drawn sign declaring their misdeeds for the world to see. From stealing socks to snaffling

Blissfully unaware of their owner's treacherous dog shaming

toilet paper or munching remote controls, even the best-behaved dogs have their moments – but don't worry, they'll be blissfully unaware of your betrayal. #dogshaming
See also MISCHIEF

DOG SHOWS

Whether you want to show off your pooch at a fancy breed show or try your luck at the local fair, there is something for everyone. Either way, make sure your fluffball can cope with the crowds and the other dogs before you take the plunge. Maybe your dog will be the proud winner of the best beard or cutest puppy award at your village fête, or perhaps you have set your sight on bigger prizes, but whatever happens, the best dog comes home with you. #bestinshow
See also PEDIGREE

Best Beard or Best in Show?

DOG SITTERS

Many owners forgo vacations where they can't take their dogs, but it is not always paw-sible and can be a big sacrifice. Luckily there are some good options to ensure a happy dog and a carefree holiday as long as you plan in advance. A friend or relation might take on your doggo – make sure they are compatible with existing pets. Then there are dog sitters who visit daily, or even move in for the duration. Asking fellow dog owners or your local vet or respected agencies for recommendations is a good place to start. If you find the right person for your four-legged pal, you can relax on your holidays knowing your pooch is in safe hands. You never know, they might even enjoy it – but you can bet you'll have the best slobbery welcome back ever.

DOG WALKERS
Walking the dog is one of life's great pleasures but sometimes our work commitments or health can get in the way. If you need to leave your dog regularly for more than four hours or you can't manage the walks, a dog walker could be the paw-fect solution for you and your pup. Ask around for recommendations and be sure to check references, insurance, transport and the other canine buddies for suitability. A good walker will bond with your dog, too, but don't fear, they will never replace you! *See also* WALKIES

DOGGO
Doggolingo for a cute dog. #doggo *See also* DOGGOLINGO, FLOOFER, PUPPER, WOOFER

DOGGOLINGO
The international language of our doggo friends, used mostly on the internet, but surely a true indication of what is going on in their fluffy heads. *See also* BLOP, DOGGO, FLOOFER, WOOFER

DOORBELLS
For many dogs, the doorbell ringing or knocking on the door will trigger much excitement and barking, and this can drive their humans crazy. But it is paw-sible to teach them better doorbell etiquette so they acknowledge the bell with just a couple of barks, then you will all be happier. Training will take some patience and persistence, particularly for the more territorial dogs. As always, use positive, reward-based training and make sure you remain consistent. With

lots of practice, you should be able to crack this!
See also BARKING, DELIVERIES, LOUD
NOISES, TRAINING

DOZING

Our dopey friends are amazingly gifted at dozing off in
ridiculous spots and positions. Puppies are particularly
proficient and will fight sleep with all their might before
they find themselves drifting off mid-action, perhaps
standing up, bottom in the air, or even face-planted in
a food bowl. Some dogs doze with their eyes a touch
open and this can be a bit spooky for the uninitiated,
but it's very common!
See also DERP, LAZY, NAPS, PUPPIES, SLEEP

*Hopelessly losing the
battle against a much-
needed doze*

DREAMS

We've all seen our pups adorably twitching, whimpering and even
barking when they're in a deep sleep and studies reveal it is very likely
our dogs are dreaming, just as we do. What on earth is happening
in those furry heads is less clear, but just like us, they are probably
processing the im-paw-tant goings-on of their lives. If only they could
recount their dreams to us over breakfast!

DROOLING

Putting up with slobbery chops is unfortunately part of being a dog
paw-rent, but certain breeds, such as Bulldogs or Bloodhounds, are
more prone to drooling. There are plenty of dapper bandanas around
to soak up the worst of it and a cloth to hand is useful if you have a
big slobberer. However, drooling can also be a sign of various health
problems, so do talk to your vet if your dog's drooling is excessive or
unusual for them. *See also* AGEING, CHOPS

EARS

Whether your furry best pal has the long droopy ears of a Basset Hound, the folded tips of the Pug or the pointed ears of a German Shepherd, there is huge variety in canine ear shape from selective breeding. Dogs can rotate their ears to help them locate a sound, but the floppy ears of many breeds can restrict this talent. It can be useful to observe your dog's ear movement while you are talking to them, as those characterful ears could reveal their mind is elsewhere. Your pooch can hear much higher frequencies than humans and can even hear into the ultrasonic range, so they are aware of much more going on than we are. However, a study revealed that dogs are pretty efficient at tuning out background noise to hear you, but only when it isn't louder than your voice, so bear with them when you're out as they might not be able to hear you.

EATING

You might be lucky enough to have a pooch whose general enthusiasm for life extends to impressive gusto in the eating department. From slobbered-on kibble dispersed around the room to delightful squishy lumps of wet food strewn across the floor, some dogs' eating etiquette will give you paws for thought. To try to stop that bowl gliding across the floor, opt for a sturdy, substantial one and a good depth should ensure that more food is in the bowl or the dog – not flying across the room. Positioning it in a place with few distractions and noise should help too. Bone appetit! *See also* FOOD

ENGLISH SETTER

These fine-looking dogs are popular family pets and are said to have gentle and amiable natures. Their gorgeous floofy tummies and long, silky speckled coats are appealing to many, but they will need a fair amount of grooming to keep those locks flowing in the breeze.

ENGLISH SPRINGER SPANIEL

These bundles of energy just love to be busy and do well on the agility scene as well as being put to work in various settings. Their adorable long floppy ears, superior noses and sweet natures make them a popular pooch worldwide.

ENTERTAINMENT

There is much to entertain your doggo in the big outdoors, but what about inside? Once the puppy years are over, sometimes so are the games, and those expectant stares can say it all. Many of us have busy lives and it can be hard to know how to

The English Springer Spaniel is a su-paw-star of the agility circuit

keep your dog entertained at home. If you take the time to play with your pooch, they are more likely to settle when you really are too busy. Try out some scent games, tug-of-war, hide-and-seek or mini agility obstacle courses and keep revolving those toys to maintain the novelty factor. *See also* AGILITY, ATTENTION, HIDE-AND-SEEK, SCENTWORK, TOYS, TUG-OF-WAR, WALKIES

ENTHUSIASM

There is little more enthusiastic than a dog in this world, especially when you walk in the door. That wagging tail, joyful body and happy face are hard to beat. There are also some dogs that have seemingly endless amounts of enthusiasm for games and will want to play until your arm is literally falling off, while others bore easily. If your dog is one of these, you could try ending a game before they are tired of it and the next time they may be more enthusiastic to pick the game up again.

EXERCISE

Even if the weather is rubbish, we still have to walk our dogs, and it appears this has a big impact on our own health as well as that of our furry friends. A UK study revealed dog paw-rents were more likely to meet exercise guidelines and to engage in other exercise like running too! It seems there are lots of paw-sitive physical and mental effects to having a dog, such as lowering your risk of cardiovascular disease. If you're looking to improve your health and fitness, you won't be barking up the wrong tree by getting a canine companion!
See also DIETS, RAIN, SUNSHINE, WEATHER

EYES

We are easily manipulated by our furry friends' soulful eyes and it seems resistance is futile. Amazingly, a study has shown that our canines' eyebrows have changed through years of domestication to make their feelings crystal clear to us humans. That irresistible expression all our dogs have in their toolbox, with the inner eyebrow raised, has an instant effect on us and even seems to ensure a quicker adoption for some. Most dogs have soft brown eyes to further our helplessness under their gaze, but some breeds can display unusual colours, such as the bedazzling baby blues of the Siberian Husky.
See also WHALE EYE

Practising those big sad eyes

FAITHFUL

Some breeds have reputations for their loyalty but whether you have a pint-sized pupperino or a big old woofer, it is almost guaranteed they are always there for you, as a faithful friend should be. It is in a canine's nature to protect and stay with their pack and an im-paw-tant part of survival in the wild, so it makes sense that our dogs are hopelessly devoted to us. *See also* AFFECTION, DEVOTION, STARING

FEAR

If you have a fearful fido – whether it is other dogs, fireworks or the vets that makes them quake in their tiny boots – it's im-paw-tant to make your doggo feel safe. Fear can often display as aggression so it is vital to address it at the earliest opportunity, and there are steps you can take with a behaviourist to gradually build their confidence in situations they find unnerving. Learning to read their body language is also essential in identifying those early signs of fear.
See also AGGRESION, ANXIETY, FIREWORKS

FINNISH SPITZ

These adorable foxy dogs, cutely nicknamed Finkies, have alert ears, lovely red fur and are re-paw-tedly big extroverts who just love to bark, so you will need to keep this chatty impulse in check. They are always busy and very bright, so might bore easily but – with a firm hand and plenty of attention and exercise – they do make excellent family pets.

The foxy Finkie

FIREWORKS

Unfortunately, fireworks can cause a great deal of worry for our furry friends and are dreaded by many canine households. If your pup gets anxious or worked up, prepare in advance by making sure you have walked them earlier in the day, have made a safe den they can retreat to and shut all the doors and windows. Let them hide if they want to – under the bed or in the cupboard under the stairs are favourite spots so you may want to put a bed or blanket in there in advance. Some soothing music may also be worth a try. *See also* ANXIETY, FEAR, LOUD NOISES

FLEAS

If you have a furry friend, you are also likely to be sharing your home with a few of these pesky bloodsuckers. It is always much easier to prevent them getting established than deal with them later, so to keep them at bay, many dog paw-rents use a topical solution on the back of the neck. They should forgive you after a while, but if your dog gets really upset there are oral or collar options to try, and emerging evidence suggests tablets may be better for the ecosystem. If the flea situation gets out of hand, talk to your vet as you will need to make a plan to rid your home of the infestation as well as treating your dog.

FLOOFER OR FLOOFBALL

Dogs with plenty of floof are often referred to as Floofballs or Floofers, but these descriptive terms can be applied to any dog in the right circumstances. #floofer *See also* FLUFFBALL, PUPPER, WOOFER

A fluffball

FLUFFBALL

A term of endearment for your ball of fluff. Particularly fluffy friends include Bichon Frises and Samoyeds. #fluffball

FOOD

There is a bewildering variety of dog food available, and it can divide dog owners, but you will need to find what is right for your particular pooch. Dog food can vary a great deal in content, so shop around to get the right match for you and your dog. Making sure your pup does not overeat and head down the chonky road is often the biggest issue in deciding on the right nutrition. Raw meat is popular but do consult your vet if you're considering it, as the cons may outweigh the apparent pros.
See also CHONK, DIETS, EATING

FOX TERRIER

These smart little dogs with their characterful long faces, distinctive eyebrows and beards will need plenty of stimulation to keep them out of trouble. Their high prey drive and superior intelligence will keep you busy! They have attractive wire or smooth white coats with tan and black markings.

Anything is paw-sible for a Fox Terrier

FOXES

Why oh why must our doggies roll in fox poo? Some dogs are compelled to flop around in the smelliest droppings and it can be hard to persuade them otherwise. It could be they simply love that smell, they want to cover their own scent as if they were in the wild, or they are marking their territory. Luckily there are special shampoos available if your dog is a regular roller in the stinky stuff. *See also* BATHS, UNSAVOURY SMELLS

FRAP

Frenetic Random Activity Period, also known as the Zoomies, that crazy time in every dog's diary. *See also* DERP, ZOOMIES

FRENCH BULLDOG

These stocky little characters, affectionately called Frenchies, have become hugely popular for their cute faces, snuggly bodies and fun-loving ways. However, they can suffer significant health problems, so make sure you research the breed and choose a responsible breeder.

FRIENDS

Yes, you are your dog's best friend, but they will probably make some special relationships with other canines you encounter on your daily walks. Just like humans, sometimes they find the perfect match of temperament in another pooch and their joyful body language will say it all.

The Frenchie, a velvety ball of silliness

FUR

Our fuzzy pals have fur coats in a dazzling range of colours, textures and lengths. Fur coats are either single layered – sported by Greyhounds and Poodles, amongst others – or double-layered with a fluffy soft undercoat for extra warmth and a protective topcoat. Those with single layers shed less fur and can be less problematic for those with allergies (but saliva and dander, both allergy triggers, are still very much present). For the rest, you will likely be covered in the stuff, especially when Spring comes around, and you may need to invest in a super-powered vacuum cleaner and a pet hair tape roller. You can kiss goodbye to those chic black outfits. *See also* ALLERGY, BRUSH, COATS, FLOOFBALL

FURSDAY

It's Thursday at last and a great day to show off your favourite floofball with all their wondrous fluff on social media – tummies particularly welcome. #fursday #fluffyfursday
See also MUTT BUTT MONDAY, TONGUE OUT TUESDAY, WOOF WEDNESDAY

FUR BABY

An affectionate term for our fuzzy friends, which might sometimes be extended to other members of the furry family too. #furbaby
See also CATS, FLOOFBALL

GARDENS

A pooch-safe garden is high on most dog-owner's lists, but many dogs, particularly small ones, can live happily without gardens if they have a regular walking and toilet schedule and plenty to entertain them in the home. When bringing a new dog home, you will need to make sure you have a strong secure fence and check it for any gaps or sneaky escape routes and conduct a thorough safety check. A lawn makes a lovely spot for games and some shade is im-paw-tant for those long hot summers. You might want to consider an area for digging and be sure to keep them out of sheds full of tools and chemicals and away from ponds. *See also* DIGGING, SUNSHINE

GERMAN SHEPHERD

These fine-looking dogs were originally bred to work, and indeed many still do, so they will need lots of entertainment and exercise to keep their clever minds busy and their athletic figures in shape. Commonly called Alsatians, their handsome black and tan coats – either long-haired or short-haired – are widely recognized, and they are very popular family pets.

GERMAN SHORTHAIRED POINTER

These dogs were bred to be hunting dogs – specifically to hunt, point and retrieve – and they are consequently very high energy and of superior intelligence. You will need to be an active owner to fulfil the needs of these handsome pointers and they will thrive when given learning tasks on your adventures. They also have a very high prey drive, so be cautious around cats and other small creatures.

GERMAN SPITZ

The larger cousins of the Pomeranian, with lots of floof and high spirits guaranteed. These adorable pooches are split into the larger Mittel and the smaller Klein. They need copious amounts of grooming and there will be a great deal of fluff flying around. *See also* FLOOFER, POMERANIAN

GIFTS

It's undeniably cute when your furry friend brings you a slobbery present when you come through the door. From their fur-avourite toy to your mangled shoe, many pups just love to lay random items at your feet and quickly learn it gets your attention. You may want to swiftly replace unsuitable objects with toys and avoid reacting if it becomes a bother. The brighter pups also drop some serious hints, perhaps bringing you their lead or ball when they are bored. *See also* ATTENTION, SHOES

GOLDEN RETRIEVER

These energetic pooches with their unmistakeable golden floof are beloved the world over. They famously help people with sight loss to enjoy full lives and Goldies love nothing more than long muddy walks and being an im-paw-tant member of the family. They do have a tendency to devour any food within sight, so keep a watch on their weight.

Proudly bringing you a special gift: your own smelly sock

GOLDENDOOLE

Also known, rather cutely, as a Groodle, the Goldendoodle is a popular cross between a Golden Retriever and a Poodle, and so can vary in size and temperament. These over-sized teddy bears are high in energy and neediness, so make sure you can meet their demands before taking the leap. *See also* COCKAPOO, CROSSBREED, LABRADOODLE

GREAT DANE

Those enormous heads house big brains and these friendly giants will charm the socks off all they meet. Likely to quickly eat their way through your bank account, make sure you consider their expansive needs if you are thinking of welcoming one of these over-sized beauties into your home.

They may be goofy, but Great Danes have big brains in there

GREETINGS

Our canines manage to communicate a wealth of information in their sometimes very brief encounters with each other, through body language and scent. Signs of a greeting going well include a relaxed unrushed approach, plenty of sniffing, perhaps touching noses before progressing to a good bottom sniff. Remember that your reaction will guide them too, so try to remain relaxed and confident and they will pick up on your demeanour. *See also* ANXIETY, FRIENDS

A Greyhound showing off those expert sad eyes

GREYHOUND

These elegant hounds will give any dog a run for its money in a sad-eyes competition. The speedy gazelles of the canine world are known for their sensitive but friendly natures and make lovely pets – although the chasing instinct can remain strong so you may find you'll get fitter faster if you opt for one of these delightful babies.

GROOMING

Depending on the breed, the grooming needs of your dog can vary enormously. Those fur-iends with high floof may need daily grooming sessions while the sleeker pups will require less attention. As with most things, starting a grooming routine early in their life will help your dog accept it. You will probably have to use a professional dog groomer when it comes to hair trimming time, so ask around to get recommendations for a good one. Whilst you can try this at home and risk giving your pooch a very bad hair day, it is a lot harder than it looks, and should be approached with caution to avoid any hair-raising moments. *See also* BATHS, BRUSH, FUR, LICKING, WASHING

A grooming hit or miss? Nobody is sure.

GROWLING

The meaning of a growl can vary widely: it can be a sign of fear, stress or aggression and should be taken as a warning that they may bite. Growling should therefore never be ignored or punished. Your possessive doggo may also bring out the growls if you try to take a toy or item of food from them. You will probably also hear your pooch gently growling during play sessions, and this is ok, but pay close attention to their signals and make sure it isn't escalating. *See also* AGGRESSION, ANGER, BITING, FEAR

GUARDING

From German Shepherds, also known as Landsharks, to the Staffies and Dobies, there are plenty of imposing dogs bred to guard against human or animal intruders. Dogs and humans have a long history of working together and guard dogs will alert and act, in contrast to the smaller watch dog, who will simply let everyone know with copious amounts of barking. *See also* DOBERMANN, GERMAN SHEPHERD, STAFFORDSHIRE BULL TERRIER, WATCH DOG

GUNDOGS

This group of dog breeds includes Spaniels, Retrievers, Pointers and Setters and they were all bred originally to help hunters. They make excellent family dogs, too, but tend to be very active and like to be kept busy, so will need lots of stimulation to stay healthy and happy.

HAPPINESS

Our pups fill our lives with happiness, and it seems we are im-paw-tant for their happiness too. A study suggested that looking into your dog's eyes releases oxytocin in both of our brains and it seems dogs value touch from us even higher than treats, so giving them lots of love and attention should make your dog happier. As for human mental health, eating a healthy diet, getting the right exercise, being comfortable, mentally and socially stimulated, and well groomed can all contribute to your pooch's happiness. *See also* JOY. LOVE. OXYTOCIN. STROKES

HARNESS

There are various types of harness available for your furry pal and like everything else in the world of doggy shopping, the amount of choice can be a bit overwhelming at first. Harnesses are pre-furred by many dog parents because they allow a bit more control, particularly over dogs that pull on the lead, and reduce the strain on your pup's neck. A comfortable and well-fitting harness that does not restrict movement is a useful bit of kit for any four-legged friend. Because canine physique varies so widely, the designs do too, so having a good think about what you and your pup really need on your walks is the 'leash' you can do. Remember your dog will also need their collar in public places. *See also* COLLARS

HEAT

When your lady doggo comes into season, it's often called being 'in heat'. Your little lady may seem restless during this trying time, with lots of pacing around, and might be grumpy or clingy at times. *See also* BITCH. COURTSHIP

HERDING

From the classic Border Collie to the unforgettable Welsh Corgi, dogs bred for herding are famous around the world and loved for their superior intelligence and impressive skills. If you choose a herding dog as a pet, you will need to make sure they get the mental and physical stimulation they crave; they need to be kept busy or they'll soon be herding you around. *See also* JOBS

HIDE-AND-SEEK

A fur-avourite game for many doggos and a great way to exercise both their well-honed bods and the grey matter. If this is a new game for you and your pup, remember to keep it simple to start with, then gradually make it harder, so they don't lose interest. *See also* ENTERTAINMENT

Hide-and-seek, fun for all the family

HOUSE TRAINING

So, you have brought your new puppy home and now the fun begins. Most puppy paw-rents would agree that top of every new pup's to-do list is definitely toilet training. Unfortunately, the pup may not agree, making this one task to challenge even the most patient of us. Be prepared for a long haul. You won't have a paw-fectly trained puppy overnight, they will make mistakes and that is a normal part of the learning process. Some puppies get the hang of it quickly, perhaps in only a few weeks, while others can take much longer to master those all im-paw-tant skills. Clean up those slips up with no fuss, and

praise like mad when they get it right and you'll soon put the messy accidents behind you. As with all training, positive reinforcement – not punishment – is the way to go.
See also POOP, TOILET

HOWLING
Many of our pooches have something resembling a howl in their repertoire, but some dogs are paw-ticularly expert at howling, including Siberian Huskies and Beagles. Our pet dogs howl for many different reasons: they might be protecting their territory, reacting to music or sirens, communicating with other dogs, trying to get our attention, or suffering from separation anxiety. Puppies can learn to howl as early as seven to ten weeks, or it may take them a little longer to learn this vocalization. Cute as it is, it might drive you and your neighbours crazy if you don't teach them quickly to keep the noise down!
See also AWOO, SIBERIAN HUSKY, SINGING

House training should not involve toilet roll

HUFFING
It's a familiar noise to most dog owners and is described as a breathy bark or just an exhale of breath, perhaps with a tiny bark, and is also known as chuffing. Confusingly, this little noise is used in a variety of situations, from happiness and excitement to uncertainty or aggression, so look for those body signals to work out exactly what's going on with your four-legged friend when they make this sound.
See also COMMUNICATION, SIGHING

HUMPING

There is no doubt this can be embarrassing for everyone, especially when your dog decides to mount an unsuspecting guest in your home. This is a completely natural behaviour for our dogs and is often triggered by play and excitement. It can be hard, but try not to laugh, as this instantly tells your dog this is a great thing to quickly get your attention. If you can spot the triggers you can try to distract with a toy before the humping commences, but using basic training commands your dog has learned, such as 'sit' or 'leave it' should get this under control. *See also* ATTENTION

This doggo has got the hump

THE DOG LOVER'S A TO Z

The Velcro Vizsla never leaves your side

HUNGARIAN VIZSLA

Supremely handsome and uniquely russet-gold gundogs, known for their high energy and super intelligence. They will need lots of attention and exercise and are sometimes nicknamed Velcro Vizslas for their need to be with their parents if at all paw-sible.

HUNTING

Although many breeds have been bred specifically to assist humans in our own hunting endeavours – with a wide range of honed skills on display, from amazing tracking ability to impressive speed, or unusually shaped bodies to get down holes – most of our pet pooches have lost the range of skills needed to effectively hunt and provide for themselves. Many of us have had a giggle at our furry friend's lacklustre attempts at chasing a squirrel or harassing a passing pigeon. Dogs rarely survive for long when they are not able to scavenge near humans, so although your doggo might fancy themselves as an expert hunter, they're maybe not ready for us to stop putting the chow down just yet. *See also* GUNDOGS

ICONS

Throughout history, dogs have represented faithfulness, loyalty and protection in many cultures. Now it seems they have become celebrated icons of the internet, and often for considerably less honourable traits. From dog-shaming to clumsy slip-ups, through the zoomies and high-fives, our modern-day icons are often now applauded for their silliest and weirdest moments. As any true icon should, our joyful furballs lighten our days and lift our spirits.

IDIOCY

There is no doubt our pups can be idiotic at times. From doggedly trying to get a large stick through a too small dog flap or careering around with a basket stuck on their heads, to incessantly chasing their tails or charging headfirst into the sofa. Our furry friends are masters at playing the fool but the really idiotic thing is we love them all the more for it. *See also* DERP, INSANITY

ILLNESS

It can be hard to see your furry friend being under the weather but just like us, they are not immune to illness and you will be concerned for your paw thing. Some dogs will remain cheery and eager to please even when feeling ruff, so watch out for any changes in their behaviour or mood as well as the more obvious signs, such as a loss of appetite or vomiting, and consult your vet. Even if you're feeling worried, try to stay relaxed, as your intuitive pup will pick up on your anxiety. *See also* VETS

INSANITY

Anyone with a new puppy will tell you they can be CRAZY and the craziness often comes at the same time each day. Even older dogs can do some very silly things sometimes and the trouble they can find themselves in will never cease to amaze us, from getting coat hangers stuck on their heads to dragging a lawn sprinkler inside the house. If they can, they will. See also DERP, FRAP, IDIOCY, X-RAY, ZOOMIES

IRISH SETTER

These red-haired beauties are full of enthusiasm and love to play. Although they are said to make great family pets, they do need lots of exercise and grooming to keep their silky chestnut manes in tip-top condition.

IRISH WOLFHOUND

The enormous sighthounds are the tallest breed in the world and even if you have the space, be prepared for your whole life to change to accommodate your gentle giant. They love human company and although kind and loving creatures, they can inadvertently knock people and smaller animals over, especially when they are younger and more boisterous, so tread with care! They have the air of a wise old owl but don't have lives as long as smaller dogs and can suffer some

You can kiss goodbye to laden coffee tables if you have an Irish Wolfhound

health problems, so research their big-scale needs and find a responsible breeder if this might be the woofer for you.

JACK RUSSELL TERRIER

These little pups, with their short legs and characterful faces, are said to be strong-willed and veritable balls of energy. They are well-known for their cheeky looks and big personalities, and an experienced owner is recommended who can handle their liveliness and spirit.

The Jack Russell has a big paw-sonality in a little body

JAPANESE SHIBA INU

These chunky foxes with their beautiful plush coats and curled tails are stars of the internet, but will need plenty of early socialization in real life. They are strong, intelligent characters and although not generally noisy, will not hesitate to use the 'Shiba Scream' if they are not pleased.

A Japanese Shiba Inu, with no current need to bring out the 'Shiba Scream'

JAWS

The jaws of your Chihuahua may strike fear into your heart but bear in mind the larger a dog's head and the wider their jaw, the higher the bite force is likely to be. Some of the highest recorded, such as for the Mastiff, are not that far off a lion, so be careful not to bite off more than you can chew when choosing a new furry friend. *See also* BITING

JOBS

Whereas our feline friends won't lift a paw for anyone, our beloved doggos have actual jobs and are genuinely useful in so many ways! From detecting cancer and avalanche rescue, to parachuting in the military and fighting crime, there seems to be no end to the work our dogs can do. Whilst you may regularly question your own pup's usefulness, remember that dogs are bone-fide heroes. Unfortunately, it seems unlikely your dog will be able to contribute to the household's expenses anytime soon. *See also* GUARDING, GUNDOGS, HERDING, HUNTING, WORKING DOGS

JOWLS

The long hanging flesh around the jaws, superbly displayed by the Bulldog amongst others. An impressive pair of jowls gives a dog undeniable character, but they will need lots of loving care to keep them clean and infection free. *See also* CHOPS

A messy chops

Fill your doggo's day with joy

JOY

Dog paw-rents will testify that our best fur-iends bring us joy by the truck load. Remember to return the favour and add a little joy to your dog's day. Slow down their walk and let them sniff every little thing they want to, let them explore and roam in a safe place to their heart's content, take time to get down and play their fur-avourite game and give them that all important undivided attention they crave. *See also* ENTERTAINMENT, HAPPINESS, LOVE, NOSES, OXYTOCIN, WALKIES

JUMPING

Puppies can start jumping about in the first weeks of their life and it's a natural instinct for them. While some will wow you with their leaps and mid-air catches, the internet will show you many who can't make the all-important hop to the sofa. A lot of jumping can take its toll on your doggo's joints, and outside on the bouncy grass is the safest place to absorb the impact. A Greyhound holds the current world record for the highest jump at 191.7 cm (75.5 inches), but Spaniels and Border Collies are impressive jumpers and do well on the agility scene. *See also* AGILITY

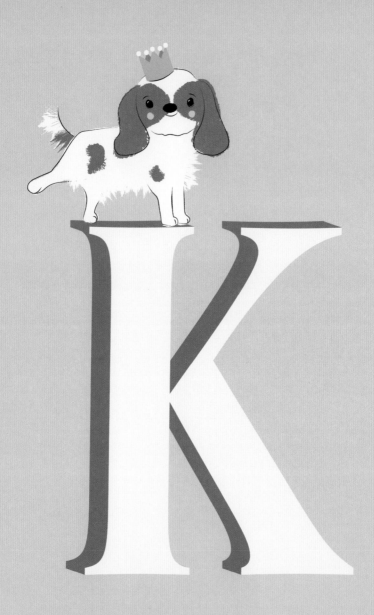

KENNELS

If you can't take your furry friend away with you or a dog sitter isn't the right option, a boarding kennel is likely to be next on your list. Ask around for recommendations and make sure you start making plans early as the best residences will get booked up well in advance. All good kennels will be licensed, clean and comfortable, and your dog will have its own roomy unit and will have daily walks outside. While flash facilities might sway you, look out for friendly staff and content dogs and don't hold back asking the im-paw-tant questions to ensure the right match for your pup. *See also* DOG SITTERS

KICKING

It's a fur-miliar routine, your dog goes to the toilet and then proceeds to vigorously kick at the grass or soil with their hind legs. It can be a bit annoying if they're kicking up your prized lawn or beloved shrubs, but this instinctive behaviour is a natural scent marking activity and, if possible, you should allow your doggo the time to complete this im-paw-tant task.

KING CHARLES SPANIEL

Not to be confused with the Cavalier Kings Charlies Spaniel, though they have much in common, these toy dogs have a flatter face with a snubbed nose and a rounded head. Be sure to research the potential health issues these little Spaniels may encounter. *See also* CAVALIER KING CHARLES SPANIEL

LABRADOODLE

A popular cross of a Labrador Retriever and a Poodle. Labradoodles can vary a great deal in temperament, appearance, and size because they are hybrids, but they tend to be on the big size, full of beans and love to play. *See also* CROSSBREED. GOLDENDOODLE

LABRADOR RETRIEVER

These stocky and charming family favourites are unfazed by most things in life, and thrive on the ruff-and-tumble of a bustling household. Labs love their food so be careful to keep these big chonks-in-waiting well exercised. Their talents and gentle natures are often put to good use as assistance dogs but their party trick is retrieving from the water.
See also GOLDEN RETRIEVER. SWIMMING

LANGUAGE

We chat to our furry pals as if they understand everything we say and frequently give them a running commentary of our day. Although much of it is probably beyond their comprehension, our dogs may pay more attention to our speech than we realize. It seems likely that domestication has selected dogs that are more in tune with human language and a study of extraordinarily gifted dogs, all Border Collies, showed that they could learn an incredible twelve new words a week and remember them for months afterwards. That baby voice that many of us adopt when speaking to our dogs has been shown to be paw-ticularly effective in getting their attention. *See also* BARK. COMMUNICATION

A lazy lump

LAZY

It can be highly amusing to observe your pooch channelling their inner sloth; maybe they've worn themselves out for the day and need some well-earned chillaxing time, or perhaps some time-out from the craziness of the household. However, there is a definite link between our own waistlines and those of our pooches, so maybe your dog is picking up on your own bad habits. Most dogs, whether they are spritely puppies or older doggos, will enjoy a walk and explore outside, and if yours is reluctant to go maybe they have some underlying discomfort. They can also get depressed, just like us, and it can be hard to summon up the energy if they are unstimulated for much of their day. Some dogs renowned for being lazy, such as Bulldogs and Pugs, might also be having trouble breathing so be sure to investigate any on-going laziness with your vet.

LEADS

There are a huge variety of leads out there for our doggos but if you are starting out with a new puppy, a soft and durable lead suitable for loose lead training with strong clip attachments is a good place to start, and extending leads are generally not useful at this point. Your pup will be very excited by the outside world and your pace may frankly be deemed not fast enough! It is im-paw-tant to start loose lead training early to ensure you are

Dropping a subtle hint with their lead

not fur-ever being dragged around town by your enthusiastic pup.
A doggo pulling on the lead is utterly exhausting for you and could
cause injuries in the long term for them – and you! You will need
lots of treats and patience to teach this skill, but you will all be much
happier when you crack it. If you are struggling to teach your pup not
to pull, you would be advised to get some help from a trainer.
See also COLLARS, HARNESS

LICKING

Anyone with a furry friend will confirm you are going to get
slobbered on. Some paw-rents love this, while others find it a tad
revolting, no matter how much they love their pooch. Dogs use their
tongues in all sorts of ways, from grooming to greeting and bonding,
and they love to explore the world with their mouths, so they need
to be able to express this natural impulse. Excessive licking could be
a sign of anxiety, so as always, pay attention to any unusual behaviour
from your pup, as with many doggo signals, it is all about the context.

LONG HAIRED

There are a variety of walking mops to
choose from, from the elegant Afghan
Hound to the charming Old English
Sheepdog or the popular Yorkshire
Terrier, but you need to know these are
high maintenance pups. They may require
frequent professional grooming as well as
a lot of daily work, so be sure to research
their needs before committing to one of
these long-haired beauties.
See also AFGHAN HOUND,
BRUSH, FUR, GROOMING

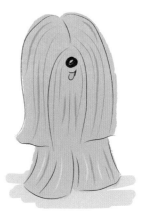

*A long-
haired
walking
mop*

LOST

It's the worst thing imaginable when your pup goes missing, but there are plenty of proactive steps you can take to swiftly get your dog safely home with you. Search your immediate local area, and double-check for smaller dogs in your home, your neighbours' gardens and sheds, and familiar places nearby. Report your dog missing to your microchip register and contact your local dog warden, rescue centres, vets, and any lost dog services in your area. Social media is a great place to quickly get the message out, with a nice clear description and photo of your beloved friend, and there are groups that assist with missing pets. Don't forget to make some posters too and ask to put them on neighbourhood notice boards. If you think your dog may have been stolen report this to the police. Hopefully the word will spread quickly, and your pup will be found safe and well and will be home with you before you know it.

Pogo was soon home thanks to this paw-ster

LOUD NOISES

It's very common for dogs to be fearful of loud noises and it can be upsetting to see our pups trembling or hiding when they are afraid. Ideally, a puppy will be introduced to a whole range of noises when they are young, from spin dryers and juicers to telephones and doorbells. You can also make use of recordings of outside sounds when your dog is nice and relaxed and gradually increase the volume from very quiet, stopping when you observe any signs of anxiety, and restarting when they are calm again. Try not to get anxious on your dog's behalf if you hear a loud noise, or your pup will think you are worried about the sounds too. *See also* ANXIETY, FIREWORKS

LOVE

There is little doubt we love our dogs, but do our pooches love us? Cynics will say your dog loves you because you feed them, but a study of street dogs showed they can quickly build loving connections with people and the bond builds faster from touch and affection than offering food. If you were to try to measure scientifically what we call love, whether through hormones, brain activity or behaviour, your dog would surely tick all those boxes! Any dog paw-rent would testify in a court that their dog loves them because, after all, we know our furry companions best.

LOYALTY

Who would question the loyalty of a canine? Whether a posh Poodle or an unrefined mutt, there is no doubt our dogs have a deserved reputation for their dependable and constant ways. We've all heard remarkable stories of courageous pups displaying steadfast loyalty in dangerous, fur-raising and challenging situations, but our everyday pooches at home are also as loyal as they come. From greeting us happily every day to waiting patiently by our sides, they always sup-paw-t us. See also DEVOTION, FAITHFUL

MANES

While a lion costume may make you chuckle, your dog may not be so amused, so let's instead celebrate the best of those that come with their own ready-to-go manes. They might be petite, but Pomeranians definitely give the Kings of the Jungle a run for their money with their floofy ruffs and assured swagger, while those chunky Chow Chows boast distinctive manes that any lion would be proud to flaunt. *See also* BEARDS, CHOW CHOW, FLOOFER, POMERANIAN

MINIATURE SCHNAUZER

A Miniature Schnauzer showing off their handsome eyebrows

These handsome little dogs with memorable bushy eyebrows, cute ears and beards are said to be great fun, loyal companions and dedicated watchdogs. They are sure to turn a few heads whilst out and about with their charming looks. Confident training will keep most mischief-making at bay. *See also* SCHNAUZER

MISCHIEF

Mangling shoes, snaffling pizza, tearing up im-paw-tant documents – all normal doggy mischief and even the most well-mannered dog will have their moments. Mischief is likely to stem from boredom, frustration or a build-up of energy with nowhere useful to go. It can be very trying at times but don't tell them off – praise and reward when they are doing the right things and distract them from their mischief making.
See also DOG SHAMING, MOON PHASES, ZOOMIES

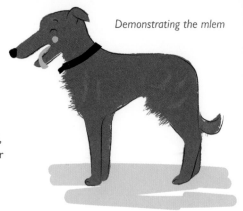
Demonstrating the mlem

MLEM
That delightful slurpy sound,
or simply the action, of your
doggo sticking out their
tongue to lick their chops.
#mlem *See also* BLOP,
CHOPS, LICKING

MONGREL
A domestic pooch of mixed or no particular breed. No less
beloved or im-paw-tant, these dogs are as unique as they come
and are likely to be healthier than their posh pedigree cousins.
See also PEDIGREE

MOODS
Our furry friends have a full range of emotions, just like we do, from
excited or happy to sad and anxious, and cannot always be expected
to be in a brilliant mood. Taking the time to read and understand
our dogs' body language can really improve our relationship. A study
revealed that dogs' personalities can change over time, just as ours
can, and that our dogs are influenced by our own life changes and
difficulties, so bear in mind that if you're having a ruff time, your
dog may well be too. Speak to your vet if your dog doesn't seem
their usual self, as illness or discomfort is sometimes not
immediately obvious to us.

MOON PHASES

Some dog parents testify to extra canine craziness on full moon nights. One study reported an increase in urgent vet visits, suggesting some additional mischief, but there is no evidence of increased aggressive behaviour from our pups. Your dog may seem more restless or alert than usual on these bright nights as there is likely to be more animal activity outside.

A mud-lover, white of course

MUD

Some dogs go crazy for the stuff and a muddy puddle is an irresistible magnet that just cannot be ignored. Dogs can get a huge amount of pleasure from playing in the mud, so let them enjoy their moment of messy bliss. You will soon be an expert in mud-management, but being prepared in advance with drying mitts, brushes and mats before they cover your home in mud will help.
See also BATHS, SWIMMING

MUTT BUTT MONDAY

It's Monday and a chance to share your snaps of your fur baby far and wide, ideally with fluffy bottoms aloft. #MuttButtMonday
See also TONGUE OUT TUESDAY, WOOF WEDNESDAY

NAMES

One of the first things our doggos learn in puppy training is to answer to their name. Ap-paw-rently if you choose a name with a vowel on the end, it is easier for your pet to pick out their name when you are speaking. A shorter name, of one or two syllables, is also advisable as they pair well with command words for speedy communication. You might want to avoid names that sound similar to commands, as they can hinder their understanding. Bear in mind your poor pup will also have to get used to the endless string of affectionate nicknames you will undoubtedly adorn them with! Choose wisely, for an embarrassing name may not be so appealing once you must shout it to the world and a moment of hilarity can cause a lifetime of pain for you and your doggo. *See also* LANGUAGE

NAPS

Our pups can fall asleep in the funniest positions during the day and whether you stumble across them flat out in the middle of the carpet, on their back with legs akimbo, drifting off while sitting up or tongue lolling elegantly out, there is nothing cuter than a dog napping. Regular napping is an im-paw-tant part of any dog's schedule but if you find your pooch is napping more than usual, do check it out with your vet. *See also* BEDS, CRATES, SLEEP

Do not disturb,
nap in progress

NEIGHBOURS

Maybe your dog barks when you are out, is a talented escape artist, or keeps causing damage without your knowledge. While no one wants to hear complaints about their beloved pooch, if your neighbours approach you about a problem with your dog, try not to get defensive and hear them out. It is your responsibility to make sure your dog is not a nuisance in your local community and to keep them restrained and safe. Many owners are worried about some aspects of their dog's behaviour, but all is not lost, and you can take steps to get them back on track with their training, however old they are, or consult a behaviourist for more complex issues. It's im-paw-tant to keep training your dog throughout their life, or bad habits can appear and can be harder to break if left too long.
See also ATTENTION, BARK, TRAINING

NEUTERING

Your over-run animal shelter will thank you for not adding to the unwanted dogs needing homes pouring through their doors, but neutering is not right for every pup. Also known as spaying for females or 'the snip' for males, this was, until recently, a rite of passage every puppy was expected to go through. But new evidence is adding nuance to the topic, and you should discuss with your vet if your doggo should be neutered and when would be the right time for them – every dog is different and your vet will be up to date with the most recent research. It is natural to be apprehensive about the procedure, but your pup will be in good hands if you decide with your vet to neuter your pup. It may have a positive impact on aggression and scent-marking, but should be avoided if you have an anxious young male until they have matured a little more.
See also CONE OF SHAME

NIGHTTIME

Dogs are not nocturnal but are particularly sensitive to things that go bump in the night and have night vision superior to our own. Just like children, our pups do well with a nighttime routine and you are all likely to get a better sleep if you stick to a regular schedule with a series of predictable signals. Make sure they have had enough exercise during the day to wear them out and give them some proper one-on-one attention before bed. Whether your pup sleeps in a crate, in a doughnut or in your own bed, consistency is im-paw-tant. *See also* BEDS, CRATES, PUPPIES, ROUTINE, SLEEP

NO

Sometimes it can feel like we are always saying 'no' to our poor pups, and while it feels very instinctive for us, it can be a very confusing word for them, especially as we usually shout it! Often your dog will have no idea what they have done wrong, when to you it is blindingly obvious, because the word 'no' is used in all sorts of mystifying situations. Instead of constantly saying 'no' to your dog, try using positive commands to direct them to do what you do want, such as 'sit' or 'give', and hopefully you will both be a lot less frustrated!

See also MISCHIEF, TRAINING

Someone is in for a ruff nighttime with this alert pup

*Norfolks: sometimes lovingly
known as little 'demons'*

NORFOLK TERRIER
These cheerful pocket-sized terriers come in smart red, black and tan, wheaten or mixed grizzle coats. They are easy to groom and are re-paw-ted to be affectionate little busy bees that may enjoy a bit of mischief.

NOSES
Cold wet noses are a fur-miliar sign of a healthy pet, although a few dogs do have naturally dryer noses. Dog noses are covered in a thin layer of mucus which helps with their incredible sense of smell; a wet nose also helps keep a dog cool. Your pup probably licks their nose a lot, which not only helps their sense of smell by sending scent particles into their mouth, but also gives it a good clean and keeps it moist. It is thought that dogs' noses may be thousands of times more sensitive than our own and if you imagined every object surrounding you had a scent, it may help you to get a glimpse inside your doggo's olfactory world. *See also* BLOODHOUND, DETECTION, LICKING, SCENTWORK

*The superior nose
of a Bloodhound*

*A gentle nuzzle will melt
the hardest of hearts*

NUZZLE

This gentle nudging will melt any dog parents' hearts and there is
nothing sweeter than an affectionate rub with the head from your
furball. Whether they are marking you with their scent, offering a
friendly 'hello', or a tactical 'feed me', it's hard to resist our furry
friends' soft nuzzles. *See also* AFFECTION, LOVE

OBEDIENCE

If you have a real clever clogs on your hands, and they have quickly mastered their basic training, you might both enjoy taking it up a notch and entering a competition obedience class. With various levels to compete in, you and your dog can show off your ability to work seamlessly together to complete a series of exercises.

OLD ENGLISH SHEEPDOG

Beneath the impressive floof lies a strapping athlete, for these renowned dogs were originally bred as working sheepdogs. Like any long-haired fluffball, they have extensive grooming needs but are playful and popular family pets. There are some health issues associated with the breed, so be sure to research and find a responsible breeder.

OUTDOORS

With all the fascinating smells, new furry friends, invigorating fresh air and exciting places to explore, most dogs love being in the great outdoors, and it is important to give them access as much as you pawsibly can. Just like for us, exercising outdoors relieves stress and anxiety and keeps them in tip-top shape. Puppies will have their tiny minds blown on their first forays outside, so let them explore at their own pace, as it will be both a thrilling and frightening experience. *See also* EXERCISE, GARDENS, WALKIES

OXYTOCIN

The cuddle chemical plays a big part in our relationships with our furry friends. Stroking and playing with our pups releases the feel-good hormone, oxytocin, in our bodies and can decrease stress and help with depression. Higher oxytocin levels were also recorded in dogs after eye contact with their owners, suggesting bonding with our pet is a paw-sitive experience for both of us. *See also* HAPPINESS

PADS

Those cute leathery paw pads come in a range of colours, including black, pink, brown and white and can even be patched with more than one colour. They are made of much thicker epidermis than the soles of our feet and are excellent shock absorbers and protect from the cold. However, they can burn quite easily, so if you're unsure on those hot summer walks, best save your walk for a cooler time of the day! *See also* CLAWS, PAWS, PEETS, SUNSHINE

PANTING

A dog panting away with tongue happily hanging out after a burst of doing doggy stuff is a fur-miliar scene and it is the main way our furry friends regulate their body temperature. During or after exercise, when they are hot or even excited, panting is perfectly normal, but excessive or heavy panting should not be ignored, as they could be overheating, having trouble breathing, or suffering from stress. *See also* BLOP, TONGUE OUT TUESDAY

PARKS

A carefree run around in the park is the highlight of many dogs' day and some off-lead fun is so im-paw-tant for your dog's physical and mental wellbeing. Plenty of parks allow you and your doggo to enjoy the space off-lead but your pooch must have great recall before you let them off-lead. Bear in mind some people find dogs intimidating, especially when they are roaming free, so make sure you have your furry friend under control. It is also essential to teach your pup some manners to make sure those all-important doggy encounters go smoothly. Watch out for dog-free zones and on-the-lead areas too. *See also* FRIENDS, OUTDOORS, SOCIALIZING

PATROL

Many dogs love to paw-trol the border of their gardens, so you might want to leave a gap between your shrubbery and fencing to allow them to complete this essential dog's job without trampling over your favourite begonias. #pawtrol *See also* GARDENS

PAWS

Although we might rightly worry about their feet in extremely wintry conditions, a dog's paws are well protected from the cold ground by a network of tightly-packed blood vessels which minimizes heat loss. You might also notice your dog gets sweaty paws, as this is one of the few unfurry places on their bodies to let sweat evaporate and help cool them down. Your pup may also get a case of clammy paws when they are stressed, just like we do. Dogs may well have a favoured front paw, for performing those all im-paw-tant tasks, but whether they are a rightie or leftie seems to be more variable than amongst us humans. *See also* PADS, PEETS, SHOES

Those irresistible peets

PEDIGREE

While there are many charming mongrels out there needing homes, you may have your heart set on a pure-bred, but be sure to research the physical and behavioural needs of the breed before you make any decisions. You may find the pooch you are after at a rescue centre as many breeds are more demanding than people realize and can end up in shelters because their owners cannot cope with or afford their needs. Some breeds are particularly prone to inherited diseases and health issues, while others are generally healthy, but all dogs, just like us, do encounter health problems. Finding the right breeder is well

THE DOG LOVER'S A TO Z

worth the time and effort. Many prospective dog owners look to breed temperaments and personalities when choosing their doggo – such as friendliness with humans and retrieving – and that is a good place to start as some characteristics are inheritable behavioural dispositions. However, a large study of dogs revealed breed is not as important as many think. All dogs are individuals and personality is also heavily influenced by experience and environment. Just as for us humans, a nurturing environment and good training can influence a dog's paw-sonality, which is affected over time and with experience. *See also* ADOPT. CROSSBREED. MONGREL

PEETS
An affectionate word for those big soft loveable paws. #peets

PEKINGESE
These little bodies house big personalities, and deep beneath all that floof are surprisingly robust frames. Pekes are known for their characterful rolling walk and will not take kindly to being rushed. Their short muzzles can cause breathing difficulties, so a responsible breeder who understands their health issues is essential. Those impressive coats will need lots of care, too.

The super-floofed Pekingese

PETTING
When meeting a new furry friend, before jumping right in to shake paws, invite them to come to you first. If their body language is open, relaxed and friendly, and they are wiggly or nuzzling you, they are likely ready for some petting, but do check with their paw-rent first.

Many dogs like to be petted on their chest, shoulders and the base of the neck, so these are good places to start but do watch their body language for signs they don't like it or have had enough. A slow and steady stroke is generally more welcome than patting. *See also* BELLY RUBS, OXYTOCIN, STROKES

PLANTS
Although our pups love exploring the outside world, unfortunately they can't be trusted not to investigate all those exciting new things with their mouths! Many plants are mildly or extremely poisonous to dogs, so be sure to check your garden for toxic greenery if you are bringing home a new furry friend and keep houseplants out of reach. If you suspect your pooch has eaten a poisonous plant, contact your vet immediately. *See also* GARDENS, OUTDOORS, TOXIC

PLAY
Every doggo has their fur-avourite games – whether it is jumping through sprinklers, playing tug-of-war, ripping toys to shreds, catching balls, or wrestling with the cat – and play is an essential part of every dog's life. Some dogs are hard to please and it can be tempting to throw money at the problem, but often some quality one-to-one time with your pooch is all they need. Doggos are

Water play, paw-fect for a hot day

very food motivated, so games involving food hunts and puzzle feeders are always a winner. *See also* BALLS, CATS, TUG-OF-WAR

POINTER

Sometimes known as the English Pointer, these handsome and elegant dogs are often spotted on art gallery walls. The name says it all as these dogs were bred to find and point at game, requiring muscular bodies that will need plenty of exercise.
See also GERMAN SHORTHAIRED POINTER

POMERANIAN

Despite their cutie pie looks, these balls of floof are said to be a tiny force to be reckoned with. Poms' high energy, potential yappiness and apparent stubbornness will need consistent training and, of course, all that fluff will need lots of brushing.

POOCH

Our pre-furred slang for doggo.
See also DOGGO, FLOOFBALL, FLUFFBALL, WOOFER

POODLE

These famously posh pooches come in three handy sizes – Standard, Miniature and Toy – and are now often mixed with other breeds to produce the popular

Don't let the floof fool you, Poodles are as sharp as they come

designer crosses, such as Cockapoos and Labradoodles. Despite the distracting floof, which may be amusingly trimmed, Poodles are of super intelligence and rather athletic. Since they have hair rather than fur, they do not shed all over the furniture.

See also COCKAPOO, CROSSBREED, LABRADOODLE

POOP

One of the least fun bits of being a dog paw-rent is dealing with the poop, but you soon learn to become a skilled su-poo-visor. If you can't bear to get down there, you could consider adding a pooper scooper to your doggy paraphernalia. Poo should be well bagged and put in an appropriate dog waste bin. A greener option is to invest in a wormery and make compost from the biodegradable bags and poo. It may give you paws for thought but it's worth the extra effort. A bit like reading the tea leaves, there is also much to learn about gut health from your dog's poo!

PREY

While most of our doggos don't need to hunt these days, bear in mind that many were originally bred to chase, retrieve or catch prey. Some breed groups, including hounds, gundogs and terriers have particularly high prey drives, but all dogs can exhibit this natural instinct. Some pooches are rather too enthusiastic, and it may put their own safety, or that of other animals and even humans at risk, so it's important to take steps to control this behaviour if the instinct overrides their training and recall. *See also* BALLS, BIRDS, CATS, RECALL, SQUIRRELS, TRAINING

PUG

Beloved by their owners, Pugs are friendly and adorable little characters, and most commonly have a smooth tan coat with a distinctive black face. The short noses and tails that they are so famous for can unfortunately bring health problems, so do your research before deciding on one of these toy dogs and, as always, choose a responsible breeder.

PUPPER

Another cute term for a puppy or dog. *See also* DOGGOLINGO

PUPPIES

If you are busy preparing for the arrival of your first puppy, do bear in mind that you will never truly be prepared and you are in for a ruff ride! These little terrors are going to exhaust you, infuriate you, challenge you and, of course, melt your heart. When you bring home a new puppy those first nights are going to be fun for the whole household and you need to be prepared to lose some sleep, much as you would if you brought home a new baby. Start as you mean to go on and make sure they get plenty of exercise, lots of playtime and that all im-paw-tant nap time. It does get better, we promise.

Puppies are generally asleep or causing chaos

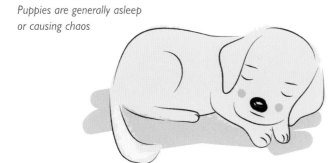

QUADRUPED

Our four-footed furballs are obligate quadrupeds, meaning they are obligated to walk on all fours. However, some little charmers like to wow us by standing on their back legs, perhaps even doing a little dance for us. While this is undoubtedly amusing, their back legs and spine are not designed to bear their weight in this way, so make sure they don't overdo the comedy; and remember, it isn't a good idea to encourage it.

QUALITY

Whether your pedigree is 'show quality' or 'pet quality' will depend on how well they meet the standards set for their breed and a show-quality puppy is likely to have a higher price tag. In our eyes, however, all dogs are quality. *See also* DOG SHOWS, PEDIGREE

QUARRELS

If you have a multi-pet household, whether it is all dogs or perhaps a cat or two, there are going to be some squabbles at times. There will be some tussling and grumbling over bowls, toys, beds, treats, those precious socks someone has snaffled, and the all im-paw-tant cuddles with you! Make sure all your pups get individual attention and have their own beds, food and water. It is recommended that you feed them separately, even if they get along, to avoid issues. Although we see lots of pets getting along famously on the internet, there are no guarantees your beloved pets will be fur-iends. Just like us, they may have completely different temperaments and find the other one's boundless energy really annoying. Minor disagreements and petty quarrels are generally harmless and perfectly normal ways our doggos communicate, but if they fight and there are injuries, do separate them and take advice from a behaviourist! *See also* CATS, FRIENDS

RAIN

Bar the odd shower-lover, most pooches are not big fans of the rain. It's miserable being out in the cold and wet but it's im-paw-tant they still get that precious exercise, so you need to push through the gloom. If your dog is happy and willing to sport one, you could consider a raincoat to protect them from the worst of it. *See also* BATHS, MUD, WEATHER

RAINBOW BRIDGE

A mythical place where our dogs will go and wait paw-tiently for us when they leave this world. We're not crying… you're crying. #rainbowbridge

RASCAL

A word strongly associated with our mischievous canines and even frequently used as a name. Be careful the name doesn't become self-fulfilling! Puppies are almost 100 per cent rascal. *See also* MISCHIEF, PUPPIES

RECALL

Before you let your pooch loose in the world for some off-lead fun, you need to know that they will come back to you when you call, to keep them and everyone else safe. Building a reliable recall with your pup takes time and patience. Coming back to you needs to be highly rewarding and fun and whether they get their favourite treats or a lovely big fuss from you, your dog need to associate returning with great things. *See also* PARKS, PREY

A pup bathing in the glow during the celebration of Kukur Tihar

RELIGION

Dogs have a range of roles in religions around the world and they are often associated with faithfulness and protection. Our pups even enjoy their own special day during the five-day Nepalese Hindu festival of Tihar. On the second day of the celebrations, dogs are the stars of the show and are blessed with a Tika, a red mark on their foreheads and adorned with pretty flower garlands. We all privately worship our own doggos, of course. *See also* ICONS

RESCUE

It's not just strays that need our help, sadly beloved pets can end up in rescue centres for many reasons, including changes in the family, not being able to cope with behavioural problems, the development of allergies, money worries or issues with accommodation. Pet charities and shelters are frequently able to offer support and advice to find an alternative solution, so if you are facing this hard decision, do seek help first. Sometimes there is sadly no other option but to find a dog a new home and rescue centres are careful not to judge. #adoptdontshop #rescuedog *See also* ADOPTION, AGEING, ALLERGY

ROTTWEILER

Their scary reputation sometimes precedes them but with good training and socialization these fine-looking dogs are said to be calm and devoted. Ideal for an experienced owner with plenty of space, Rotties are held in high regard by those who know and love them, and they are even re-paw-ted to have a derpy side.

ROUTINE

Our fluffy pals thrive on a constant and fur-miliar routine, as it brings a sense of security to their little world. It can really help with anxiety and behaviour issues if your dog knows what to expect and when it will happen in their day. If your pup doesn't already have a routine, make a plan that will work for both of you that includes a regular and predictable schedule for feeding, walking, playing, training, naps and bedtime. Our own days can vary more than our doggos, so try to keep it consistent for them if at all paw-sible. *See also* ANXIETY, BEDTIME

RUNNING

Even the laziest of our furry friends has a variety of gaits in their repertoire, from the walk and amble through to the speedier trot, canter and gallop. It won't surprise many dog paw-rents, who know full well the joy a good run-around brings their fur baby, but a study revealed our pooches experience a similar runner's high to humans. *See also* EXERCISE, HAPPINESS, JOY

The Greyhound wins paws down at running

SAMOYED

These stunning snowy fluffballs have permanent smiles which befit their happy-go-lucky natures. Samoyeds are very active and will need copious amounts of exercise and a great deal of grooming. If you can give them the company they love and put up with the white floof everywhere, they make charming members of the household.

SCENTWORK

Our dogs just love to put their superior noses to good use, so you can brighten their day with some stimulating scent games, which are particularly helpful for those high-energy super-brains. Simple hide-a-treat games with closed fists or cups, or hide-and-seek with you or a fur-avourite toy are great ways to entertain and tire out your four-legged friend. There are also nosework classes around if you want to up your pup's skills and they can be great fun for you both.
See also COMMUNICATION, ENTERTAINMENT, GREETINGS, NOSES, SNIFFING

SCHNAUZER

Just like the Three Bears in *Goldilocks*, Schnauzers come in Giant, Standard and Miniature sizes. The name derives from the German word *schnauze*, meaning snout, and you can see why with their unmistakeable beards. These are clever dogs that love to be busy.
See also MINIATURE SCHNAUZER

SCRATCHING

If you notice your pooch is scratching more often than usual and you are up to date with their flea treatment, you should talk to your vet. Although fleas are often the cause, there are various allergies and skin infections that can also make life miserable for your pup, so these should be properly investigated by a dog-tor. See also FLEAS

SELFIE SUNDAY

An op-paw-tunity to show the doggo community your lovely face alongside your probably far more photogenic pup. #selfiesunday *See also* MUTT BUTT MONDAY, TONGUE OUT TUESDAY, WOOF WEDNESDAY

SERVICE DOGS

Our furry heroes have many vital jobs assisting humans with their day-to-day lives. From the familiar guide dogs and hearing dogs to the less widely known medical detection dogs, there are many pups doing essential work in the community who deserve a round of ap-paws for providing a lifeline for so many people. You should never pet an assistance dog while they are working with a visually or hearing impaired person, for example – after all, you wouldn't give an on-duty police officer a hug, would you? *See also* JOBS, THERAPY DOGS, WORKING DOGS

SHIH TZU

Likely to have originated in Tibet, these cute and dinky companion dogs have big personalities and ridiculous amounts of floof. If you are able to be around for most of the day and have time for daily grooming sessions, these well-built pups are said to be a great choice for a first timer but will appreciate some peace and quiet.

Small scale floof of the Shih Tzu

*An unfortunate victim
of shoe mauling*

SHOES

Any dog or puppy owner will confirm our fluffy friends' fixation with our shoes. Human footwear smells gloriously of us and features lots of interesting scents from outside, so they are bound to attract the attention of our pooches. Shoes also make excellent and easily available toys for a canine looking for entertainment, so try swiftly offering an appealing trade and lavish them with praise for choosing the new option. It is generally agreed dogs really don't need their own shoes, unless they are injured or have specific needs as working dogs, so resist the lure of those cute doggy booties, which may even cause them discomfort. *See also* MISCHIEF, PADS, TOYS

SIBERIAN HUSKY

With their characterful upright ears and striking coats, these magnificent dogs will definitely get noticed. They are said to make intelligent companions and are skilled at sled-pulling, should the op-paw-tunity ever arise. They need plenty of exercise and breeders advise they should remain on the lead in open areas, due to a tendency to run off. Although they are generally fairly quiet, they do enjoy a good howl as befits their wolf-like looks, and this may not be appreciated by the neighbours. Rather cutely, they like to snuggle their noses under their fluffy tails when having a snooze, which is affectionately known as the 'Siberian Swirl'.

*The Siberian Husky will
wolf down anything*

SIGHING

Often thought to be an exclusively human peculiarity, the sigh is also, rather amusingly, sometimes heard emanating from our fuzzy pals. Just as for humans, it generally indicates an untroubled and contented mood while your canine is relaxing or snoozing, but it can also be a sign of boredom or unhappiness. Your cunning canine may also learn their dramatic sighs quickly get your attention, so try to ignore them if this is the case. Sighing accompanied by moans, groans, or other noises could be a health or anxiety issue, so as always, do pay attention to their body language. *See also* ATTENTION, COMMUNICATION, HUFFING

SINGING

The internet is awash with adorable doggos enjoying their moment in the spotlight, happily singing along to all manner of tunes. Although any dog can find a diva within, Huskies, Malamutes and Samoyeds are more likely to join in with a sing-along ap-paw-rently. A study showed dogs are more chilled listening to classical music than pop but tend to make more noise listening to metal. If your pooch is busy howling away to the music, make sure they are enjoying the fun, and not communicating their disapproval of the racket. *See also* BARK, COMMUNICATION, HOWLING

SIRE

A perhaps overly impressive sounding title for the male parent of puppies, who are mostly lacking in fatherly skills beyond the deed. *See also* PUPPIES

SIT

A classic command and one every good doggie should know. It is a great place to start training your pup and as well as being incredibly useful for keeping your dog under control and teaching them good manners, it is very satisfying and easy to master. Some chilled-out dogs will soon lie down if asked to sit for a while, just as you will gradually slide into a slump on the sofa.
See also TRAINING

This doggo has paw-sitively mastered the Sit command

SLEEP

According to one survey of paw-rents, eight out of ten of us will compromise our own sleep for the sake of our furry friend. From lying all night long in an awkward position for fear of waking our beloved pooches, to shivering without a cover while they hog the duvet, it seems many of us frequently put our best fur-iends needs above our own! If you share your bed with your furball, as many ap-paw-rently do, be careful your hairy friend doesn't overheat in those thick covers designed for furless humans. Puppies need around twenty hours of sleep a day, which is really important for their brain development, so don't worry if they are snoozing a lot.
See also BEDS, BEDTIME, NAPS, NIGHTTIME

SMOL

Those cute little toy dogs are very smol indeed. Whether
you want a powder puff Pomeranian or a cheeky
Chihuahua, there are plenty of small dogs to choose
from. #smol *See also* TOY DOGS

SNIFFING

Having a good sniff is an essential part of any doggo's
day and however frustrating it can be sometimes,
take a few moments to let your dog explore those fur-
avourite places with their twitching noses. Sniffing gives
them information about the world around them, other
dogs and creatures, and is a very stimulating and rewarding
activity for them. It is a great way to keep those high-energy,
super-brained breeds content with minimal effort from you!
See also DETECTION, GREETINGS, JOY, NOSES,
PETTING, SCENTWORK

SNOOT

An adorable nose, which might be highly boopable. #snoot
See also BOOP, NOSES

SOCIALIZING

When you welcome a new puppy into your life, socialization will
be a word you hear a lot and it is really important to make this a
paw-sitive experience for your pupper. Choosing to buy your pup
from a responsible breeder is the best way to get this process off to
a good start and is well worth the wait. The first sixteen weeks of a
pupper's life are the most important for socialization and habituation.

Taking your puppy out in a sling and observing people from a distance is a good way to gradually introduce them to the exciting world of humans. Take this at your pup's pace, don't force them to do anything they are not ready for. Find a well-run puppy class to add other dogs to the mix. One that focuses on you and your pup in a safe environment with other puppies present is the best approach, and it's a good idea to give puppy parties and big play sessions a wide berth. Some well-chosen walks or interactions with a calm adult dog are also im-paw-tant. *See also* FRIENDS

SOCKS

You may well have a sock thief in your household and our fluffy footwear seems to hold an irresistible allure for many pooches. Whether they stash them in their beds or drool all over them, your socks smell captivatingly of you and snaffling them will often get your attention. It's best to avoid temptation and keep them out of their way if paw-sible, and should your dog actually consume a sock, do call your vet for advice! *See also* SHOES, X-RAY

A proud sock hoarder

SOFAS

Our couches are, by design, one of the comfiest places in the home and our doggos are fully aware of this. Some owners do not want their dogs on the sofa at all, while others paw-sitively welcome the company and snuggle time. A useful compromise could be having a blanket specially for your dog on the sofa. It's really im-paw-tant to be consistent and to make sure everyone in the household follows the same rules, or your furry friend will be very confused.

SPANIEL

Spaniels are popular and energetic gundogs and are known for their long floppy ears and silky-smooth coats. *See also* CAVALIER KING CHARLES SPANIEL, COCKAPOO, COCKER SPANIEL, ENGLISH SPRINGER SPANIEL, KING CHARLES SPANIEL

SPITZ

Spitz breeds have beautiful thick coats that are often white, and their pointed muzzles and upright ears give them an unmistakeably foxy or wolf-like look. *See also* FINNISH SPITZ, GERMAN SPITZ, POMERANIAN, SAMOYED

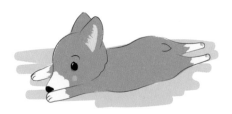

SPLOOT

Doggolingo for lying tummy down with legs splayed out cutely on the floor, sometimes paw-ticularly associated with the Corgi. #sploot

A Corgi elegantly demonstrating the sploot for us

SQUIRRELS

These little furries are beyond exciting and their cheeky ways can be infuriating for some of our doggos. Chasing gives our dogs a thrill that's hard to match and the more they do it, the harder it is to control. It's best to train your dog as a puppy not to chase the little critters, but it is paw-sible to get control when they are older and more set in their ways too. As well as training, you will need to find other ways to fulfil their chasing instincts and boost those endorphins with challenging scent games and play. *See also* BIRDS, PREY, RECALL

ST BERNARD

These enormous dogs are famous for the daring Alpine rescues of their past and often amusingly depicted with brandy barrel at the ready. Their huge size can bring health problems and taking on the challenges of a super-sized Bernie is not for the faint-hearted, but they are certainly the gentle giants of the dog kingdom.

STAFFORDSHIRE BULL TERRIER

Due a reappraisal, the loveable Staffie

Widely loved and feared in equal measure, the Staffie is a well-built and powerful dog with a loving nature that will make an adorable pet with the right training and socialization. Unfortunately, there are lots of Staffies in rescue centres seeking loving homes, but they are often easy to train, generally healthy and simple to groom, so can be great pets for families – those that know their true natures sing their praises.

STARING

Our furry friends are rather prone to staring at us and sometimes you might not know why. They might be trying to figure out what is going on by reading your body language. Or they could be after something, whether it is some of your tasty dinner or your undivided attention. Or they could simply be expressing their affection. The cutest quizzical slant of the head or those big adoring eyes can be hard to ignore, and more im-paw-tantly, they don't half know it! *See also* AFFECTION, EYES, WALKIES

STICKS

We've all seen a doggo proudly lugging a stick ten times their size and it seems to satisfy some deep-set instinct. Dogs love of sticks is a cultural given and while they can be a source of great fun on their outdoors adventures, unfortunately injuries while catching and chewing sticks can and do happen, so it is generally safer to choose a rope toy or ball for your pooch to retrieve. *See also* BALLS, BONES, OUTDOORS, TOYS

Big or smol, sticks are magnets for all dogs

STRETCHING

The pleasures and benefits of stretching cross the species and many dogs like a good stretch throughout their day. While they are maybe not quite as graceful as those bendy felines, they are efficient at flexing their muscles, perhaps after a snooze or before a burst of doggy activity. They may even join in with their human when they are limbering up. *See also* SPLOOT

STROKES

Anyone that has spent quality time with a dog will confirm the pleasure of stroking our furry friends is surely good for us. A study backed this up by revealing that stroking our pooches engages the part of the brain responsible for social and emotional interactions, and elicited more emotional arousal than by merely stroking a cuddly toy. *See also* BELLY RUBS, OXYTOCIN, PETTING

STROLLER

The doggy stroller is now a common sight in our parks and streets, and they are a useful piece of kit if you have a small dog. They are also a great way to get your senior pup or a dog with mobility problems, whether temporary or on-going, outdoors in the fresh air and getting some much-needed stimulation. When you're choosing a stroller, be sure to check the weight limit and size is right for your precious pooch and check the safety features. You can even get buggies for multiple dogs if you have more than one furry friend to wheel around. *See also* EXERCISE, TOY DOGS

STUD

Your furry boy may fancy themselves as a bit of a stud, but in this case neutered males need not apply. Whether your dog would make a good stud depends on their health, fertility and temperament, and they'll need to be fully health-tested and screened to make sure they can produce healthy, happy pups. See also HEAT, NEUTERING, PUPPIES, SIRE

STUBBORNNESS

Many of us think our furballs have a stubborn streak, and it can sometimes feel like they have set out to drive us crazy and many of us will affectionately paint our dogs with the stubborn brush. Stubbornness can be attributed to all kinds of inconvenient behaviour and putting it down to wilfulness doesn't really help you get to the bottom of the problem. Every dog is an individual and they have different needs and desires, and some will need more work from you in their training. Getting to know your dog and reading their body language along with consistent training throughout their life is a big part of your job as a paw-rent. Like humans, dogs have a variety of personality traits, whatever their breed, but some breeds are re-paw-ted to be a little more stubborn than others.

See also ANTHROPOMORPHISM, COMMUNICATION, MISCHIEF

A stubborn furball

THE DOG LOVER'S A TO Z

SUNSHINE

Just like for us humans, exposure to sunlight can be good for our heat-loving doggos' physical and mental health and is relaxing and soothing. However, dogs can also get too much sun and can overheat easily with all that fluff, so be sure to watch them carefully for signs of heat stroke, sunburn and dehydration. Your pup may need some doggy sun-cream for their vulnerable patches of skin, such as their ears and noses, particularly if your dog is pale-coloured. In hot weather it is best to keep walks for the early morning and late evening. Plenty of shade, frozen toys, supervized paddling pool sessions and sprinklers can be helpful to keep your pup cool. If your dog does get heat stroke, quickly covering them in cold (not tepid) water and actively cooling them with something like a fan before heading to the vets can be a lifesaver. *See also* GARDENS, PADS, PANTING, PLAY, SWIMMING, WATER

SWIMMING

Some dogs were literally born to swim and were bred for water jobs, such as Labrador Retrievers and Portuguese Water Dogs, and even have long toes and webbed feet that make swimming a breeze. Your pup might enjoy a dip in the water, whether it is paddling in a stream or fully immersed in a park pond, but not all dogs are natural swimmers. Some breeds, paw-ticularly stocky breeds or those with short snouts such as Pugs and Bulldogs, may find it difficult, so be cautious around water. All dogs – even those excellent swimmers – should be supervised in the water. *See also* JOY, SUNSHINE, WET DOG WEDNESDAY

TAILS

Doggy tails vary greatly in length and can consist of anything from six to twenty-three bones. They also come in a bewildering number of types, from the bobtail and brush to the corkscrew and crank, or the sabre and scimitar to the wheel and whip. Tails are, of course, an im-paw-tant balance and communication tool and dogs with short, curly or cropped tails don't have the same ability to use them to convey their feelings, but they are generally able to use the rest of their body to make up for it. *See also* WAGGING

TASTE

It may still surprise you that our canine friends have a much less refined sense of taste than we do. However, they redress it with their superior noses – most doggy foods are not all that in the taste department but are loaded with exciting smells that walk a perilously thin line between being yummy to dogs and absolutely disgusting to us. *See also* EATING, FOOD, TREATS

TEETH

Our unlucky pups will teethe twice in a short space of time, and it can leave you with an irritable and drooly new friend. Adult dogs have an impressive forty-two teeth, including four of those all-important canines. Dogs can encounter lots of teeth problems, just as we do, and will benefit from regular brushing with a doggy toothpaste and brush. It amuses some when their seemingly oblivious doggo gets their lips stuck on their teefs. #teefs *See also* BITING, CHEWING, CHOPS, JAWS

Just about tolerating the toothbrush

TERRIERS

Whether you like your dogs pocket-sized, like the Cairn Terrier, or on the larger size, like the Airedale, there will be a terrier to suit you. Some have luxurious silky locks while others have short wiry coats, but all these busy bees will have plenty to say.

See also AIREDALE TERRIER, BORDER TERRIER, STAFFORDSHIRE BULL TERRIER, WEST HIGHLAND TERRIER, YORKSHIRE TERRIER

THERAPY DOGS

These furry counsellors visit and comfort people in all sorts of settings – including schools, hospitals and hospices – and even offer support after disasters, natural or otherwise. Canines can offer a cocked ear without judgement and their presence can soothe and reassure like nothing else. Therapy dogs also benefit from the interactions, if they get plenty of rest and play time, but not all dogs are cut out for the job.

Some wise and furry counsel

See also JOBS, OXYTOCIN, SERVICE DOGS, WORKING DOGS

TOILET

Even when the horror of house training is well and truly behind you, you will always be super-proud of your doggo for doing it in the right place and smugly congratulate yourself on your exemplary paw-renting skills. Puppies need to go to the toilet a LOT and ageing doggos will probably start to go more frequently too, so be sure to appreciate that bit in the middle where your dog only needs to go a reasonable three to five times a day!

See also AGEING, HOUSE TRAINING, POOP

*A derpy tongue out
Tuesday moment*

TONGUE OUT TUESDAY

It's Tuesday and a great op-paw-tunity to capture
and share your doggo looking a little derpy, with
their tongue hanging out. #tongueouttuesday #tot
See also DERP, BLOP, MLEM, MUTT BUTT
MONDAY, WOOF WEDNESDAY

TOP DOG

Although we've thankfully moved on from the top-dog dominance
theory, and we can rest easy knowing our pooches are not busy
conspiring to overturn us at every available op-paw-tunity, your dog
will surely always be top dog in your eyes?

TOPKNOT

For those pooches with copious amounts of face hair that gets in
their eyes, you might want to try a topknot. These fancy ponytails
perched cutely on top of the head, perhaps embellished with a bow,
are modelled most frequently by Shih Tzus, Yorkshire Terriers and
Toy Poodles. If you can get your pooch to sit still, after brushing you
can use a soft parting comb to separate the hair from the corners
of the eyes and gather it gently on top.
Secure with a doggy hairband and loosen
a little to make sure it isn't pulling on
their eyes. Easy! Or not, depending on
your furry friend's mood that day.

*A Yorkie modelling the top
knot in all its glory*

TOXIC

Unfortunately, our clever pals can be rather unwise when it comes to hoovering things up and there are plenty of dangers lurking in the home, garden and further afield to contend with. From human fur-avourites such as chocolate and alcohol to onions, corn on the cob, avocado, grapes, raisins, macadamia nuts and artificial sweeteners, there are a surprising number of foods to avoid. There are also medicines, household cleaners and poisonous plants to contend with. Therefore, make sure you do your research before you bring home a pup so you can make your home and garden pup-resistant, putting anything hazardous out of reach or in a locked cupboard, to prevent the unthinkable. Do remember, though, that nothing is 100 per cent puppy-proof so you'll also need to keep your wits about you.

TOY DOGS

These mini puppers make up for their small stature with plenty of personality and va va voom. This group includes the fuzzball Bichon Frise, the lively Papillon, and the mischievous Affenpinscher amongst many others. A bone-us of living with a toy dog breed is they often don't need as much exercise or space as a bigger dog but there are exceptions, such as the Italian Greyhound. *See also* BICHON FRISE, CAVALIER KING CHARLES SPANIEL, CHIHUAHUA, POODLE, PUG, SMOL

The Papillon makes up for its small stature with sizeable ear floof

TOYS

Our doggos are always on the lookout for an exciting new toy, whether it is your socks, coveted cuddly toys or your guest's shoes, and we dog paw-rents spend huge amounts of our hard-earned cash trying to find the perfect toy to entertain our insatiable pets. Fur-avourites to look out for include treat and kibble puzzles that can give them a mental and a dental work out, tug ropes, chews, stick toys, doggy blowing bubbles and of course, you can't beat a classic ball. Although some toys aim to keep your doggy busy without you, playing with you is always going to be the best game around. *See also* BALLS. CHEWING. ENTERTAINMENT. SOCKS, SHOES

Don't get between this Rottie and his fluffy bunny

TRAINING

While we all aspire to a flawlessly trained pooch, life (or a wilful pup) sometimes gets in the way, and there is no doubt that training takes hard work and perseverance, but it is well worth the effort. You and your pooch are going to be much happier and work together effectively as a team with good positive training and you'll be more confident in all kinds of environments and situations. No dog or paw-rent is perfect, of course, and you may have to go back to basics sometimes to remind you both of their training. You will also need to keep it going throughout their lives. *See also* AGILITY. BITING. HOUSE TRAINING. NO. OBEDIENCE. RECALL. SIT. SOCIALIZATION

TREATS

Finding the treat that really motivates your pupper and gets that tail wagging can be a vital part of the puzzle of successful training. There is, of course, a bewildering array of treats out there to entice you and your furry friend, and finding the right one for your pup can take some shopping around. Smelly treats can work wonders and ones that you can hide easily in your hand are useful for training. Which treats are deemed extra yummy by your pup will depend on their own fur-avourite tastes, textures and smells but watch out for those doggy calories and make sure you factor in the extra intake in their daily diet, or you could soon end up with a chonk on your hands! Remember, too, that high-value rewards can also be praise, toys and play. *See also* BONES, CHONK, DIETS, HAPPINESS, TASTE, TRAINING, TRICKS

TRICKS

Amaze your dog-less friends by teaching your pooch some easy tricks that are fun for you both to master. From shaking paws to fur-iendly waves, high fives and kisses on demand, after your dog has got to grips with their basic training, there are lots of amusing tricks to entertain your guests with. Positive reinforcement is always the way to go, so treats are your best fur-iend here.

Tricks will astound your chums

TROUSERS

The question of how a doggo would wear
trousers or pants consumed the internet for
a sweet moment. Would they sport them
on their back legs or on all four legs? Whilst
extensive scientific tests conclude they look
better just on the rear, there are ap-paw-rently
actual doggy trousers out there to cover all
four legs, no matter how amusing they may
look. *See also* ACCESSORIES, COATS

TUG-OF-WAR

A fur-avourite game for many doggos and fun for their human friends
too! Whether you use a rope toy or a rubber ring, this entertaining
game gets some dogs very excited. Your pooch will need to have
the 'leave' command mastered first, so you can keep control of the
game (or is that cheating?!). Remember to praise them a lot and
stop the game from time to time to keep their excitement under
control. Short bursts of fun work a treat and it is a super way for
human and doggo to bond. *See also* BALLS, ENTERTAINMENT,
GROWLING, TOYS

*A paw-some game
of tug-of-war*

UNDERDOG

Every rescue centre has a few of these, waiting paw-tiently for their fur-ever home. Whether they have medical needs, take a little longer to make friends, or have very specific requirements, some dogs can be hard to find new homes for. No less loveable than the others, maybe one of these underdogs could be the paw-fect match for you? *See also* ADOPTION, RESCUE

UNSAVOURY SMELLS

There is no doubt our beloved dogs can, just like us, be a bit whiffy from time to time. Maybe they are guilty of rolling in some lovely fox poo, or the dreaded time for a bath has come around, but there are numerous health problems that can lead to a stinky pooch. Skin problems, ear infections and dental disease are particularly common causes of unpleasant odours emanating from your doggo, so speak to your vet if the stench is not going away. *See also* BATHS, FOXES

URBAN

If you live in the big city, you might want to choose a pooch that is going to be tolerant of crowds, is relatively easy to train, on the quiet side and has a friendly nature. Smaller pooches are generally well suited to an urban lifestyle, particularly if you live in an apartment. It is im-paw-tant to research before you decide but if you have a loving home and access to green spaces, many dogs will thrive regardless. Some popular breeds for apartment dwelling include Shih Tzus and Basenjis. *See also* PARKS, SMOL, TOY DOGS

VARMINTY

A varmint is basically an animal up to no good, but varminty is often applied to terriers and affectionately describes their spirited and up for pretty much anything expression. Most of our dogs have something varminty about them, we're sure you'll agree.

VEGAN

With eco concerns on many minds, the debate over whether our pets can go vegan has hit the headlines and can divide dog lovers. While canines are omnivores, they do love their meat, and while theoretically they could obtain all their nutritional needs from plants, some argue that it is cruel and many vets are concerned by the lack of research on the long-term effects on health. If not carefully curated with certified veterinary nutritionist advice, a vegan diet could quickly cause ill-health. Whatever the future for our dog's diets, quality and nutritionally-complete food is essential for their health, as well as yumminess for their wellbeing. Insect protein diets could be a better alternative whilst the jury is out on vegan diets.

See also DIETS, FOOD

VETS

Our brave boys and girls generally do not appreciate a visit to the vets. They are remarkably attuned to vet-visit vibes and will likely realize where they're going before you've even shut the front door. Some will stoically accept their fate but many others will stubbornly drag their paws, desperately try to hide, burrow in your arms, or demonstrate whale eye in all its glory. You can't really blame them! However, regular checks at the vets are important for their long-term health. Plenty of reassurance from you will be needed and try not to let your own anxieties spill out. Bringing them in regularly for treats and paw-sitive associations can be really helpful.

WAGGING

A wagging tail is generally taken to mean a happy dog, but not all tail wags are equal! Tail movements vary between different breeds, but most of our furry friends can use their tails to communicate a range of emotions in different social situations. A relaxed sweeping tail suggests an untroubled canine, while a speedy circling movement, like a helicopter, is likely to indicate a doggo very excited to see you! A slow wag could mean your pooch is a little unsure of the situation, while a highly aroused dog might have a rapidly wagging tail held high. *See also* AFFECTION, ENTHUSIASM, TAILS

WALKIES

Most dogs' fur-avourite time of the day and always top of their to-do list. A word that will guarantee pricked ears, no matter how quietly you say it.

WASHING

While many pedigree pups need help with their grooming routine, dogs are also skilled at doing a little self-grooming of their own. Your dog, rather like a cat, may lick their paws and use them to clean their heads and faces and have a gentle nibble at their coats and, of course, shamelessly lick their privates clean, paw-ticularly when you have guests. *See also* BATHS, GROOMING, LICKING

WATCH DOG

A watch dog will loudly inform you when you have an intruder, but won't do much about it — that's your job. *See also* GUARDING

An ever-vigilant watch dog wannabe

Every doggo has their own paw-ticular drinking style

WATER

Some of our furry friends will elegantly lap up their water with barely a drop spilled, while others have their own special ways of getting water to mouth and may drown the surrounding area with enthusiastic abandon. Keeping your pooch hydrated is su-paw important as they can lose water fast from panting and can overheat easily. Although their standards might seem low, a nice clean drinking bowl with fresh water is essential for every doggo. *See also* SWIMMING

WEATHER

Many dog paw-rents report their sensitivity to impending weather and frequently claim their pooches can predict a storm. It could be their finely tuned noses can smell something in the air before us or sense changes in pressure that we are less sensitive to.
See also RAIN, SUNSHINE, WATER

WELSH CORGI

These clever little dogs come with the Royal seal of approval. There are two types of Corgi: the best-known Pembroke and the Cardigan, which is generally a little larger and has a longer tail. The characterful Pembroke has an adorable foxy face and fabulous big ears.

WEST HIGHLAND WHITE TERRIER

A little ball of energy and a fur-avourite companion dog. Although Westies have the sweetest of faces and a butter-wouldn't-melt innocence about them, they are still terriers at heart and will furiously defend their home and family. Some health issues are associated with the breed, so do your due diligence.

WET DOG WEDNESDAY

If you have a water-lover, you may enjoy showing them off in all their soggy glory on Wednesdays. If not, Woof Wednesday may suit you better. #wetdogwednesday *See also* MUTT BUTT MONDAY, SWIMMING, TONGUE OUT TUESDAY, WOOF WEDNESDAY

WFH

Working from home has brought joy to many doggo's days and it can be a real comfort to have your pooch for company while you toil at your desk. It does not come without its hazards, however, with confused and excited dogs demanding playtime, muscling in on your calls or yapping at the cat on the fence while you speak to the boss. If you have recently started working from home, it's a good idea to introduce a structure to your day if paw-sible. Starting your day with a lengthy walk whilst letting them sniff to their hearts content will tire your dog out for a while and boost your own mood before you start wrangling with work problems. Have treats, puzzles and chews at the ready for those tricky moments and schedule in regular play sessions when it works for you. #wfh
See also ATTENTION

A WFH take-over situation

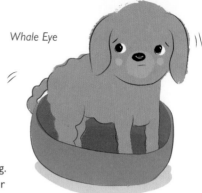

Whale Eye

WHALE EYE

Whale eye is when your furry
friend shows the whites of their
eyes, with their head turned away
a little but eyes fixed on something.
You may see this expression if your
pooch is stressed or uncomfortable
with a situation, such as being examined by a vet
or enduring an unwelcome hug from a well-meaning new friend.
Sometimes they also do this in play or when they are excited, so look
out for other body language and the situation they are in so that you
interpret accurately. *See also* ANXIETY. VETS

WHINING

Like many forms of doggy communication, whining or crying
can have various meanings and you need to have a good look at
their body language to get the right one. Puppies whine a lot to
communicate their needs, whether it's hunger, needing a wee
or urgently requiring your undivided attention! Your doggo may
whine when they are fearful or anxious, and crying could also be
a sign of pain or discomfort, so take the time to understand what
is wrong before taking action. *See also* ANXIETY. BARKS.
COMMUNICATION. LANGUAGE

WHIPPET

These soulful pups are known for their crazy antics one minute
and being a lazy bones the next. They are said to be gentle and
affectionate and while they love their exercise, they will also
appreciate their time cosying down for a nap. Re-paw-ts suggest they
like a snuggle under the duvet and they are apparently masters of the
bizarre sleeping position.

WOOF WOOF

The classic dog all-purpose bark in English. Dogs say 'wouf wouf' in France, 'woef woef' in the Netherlands and 'voff voff' in Sweden, but 'wāng wāng' in Mandarin and 'guau guau' in Spanish.

WOOF WEDNESDAY

Let's face it, pretty much anything goes on this day, but if you can capture a gentle woof, all the better. #woofwednesday
See also MUTT BUTT MONDAY, TONGUE OUT TUESDAY, WET DOG WEDNESDAY

WOOFER

Sometimes refers to a paw-ticularly large one, but it is a term that could be applied to any doggo really. #woofer
See also DOGGO, DOGGOLINGO, FLOOFER, FLOOFBALL, FLUFFBALL

WORKING DOGS

These dogs have serious work to do and are here to help us in numerous ways. The working group of breeds includes dogs bred to pull sledges, to protect and to rescue, such as the Alaskan Malamute, the Dobermann and the St Bernard. See also GUARDING, GUNDOGS, HERDING, HUNTING, SERVICE DOGS

X-RAY

Our crazy dogs are notorious for wolfing down anything, and ap-paw-rently it really doesn't matter if it's edible or not. It won't astonish many dog owners, but an annual vet's x-ray competition has revealed our less-than-clever pooches have ingested a startling series of random objects, from spoons and spatulas to plastic toys and impressive collections of rocks. A frequent cause of vet visits is foreign body obstruction, which can be very dangerous, so keep temptations out of their way and remember if they can eat it they just might. *See also* BONES, GARDENS, SOCKS, TOYS, VETS

XOLOITZCUINTLE

The characterful Xolo comes in various sizes and both coated and hairless varieties, which are also known as Mexican Hairless Dogs. They will need special care for their soft silky skin and are highly sensitive to the cold, so may appreciate a fluffy jumper.

XXL

While an enormous cuddly bear of a dog is the dream of many cynophiles, there are considerable practical and financial issues, as well as health problems, associated with the giant breeds, so be sure to research extensively before you bring a super-size woofer into your life. Obviously no XXL dog is too big for laps. *See also* CHONK, GREAT DANE, IRISH WOLFHOUND, ST BERNARD, WOOFER

YAPPER

A little doggo with a snappy bark, such as a Yorkie or Jack Russell. *See also* SMOL, TOY DOGS

Just like for us, yawning can be contagious!

YAWNS

Maybe they are just dog-tired, but yawning can be a sign of stress in our pooches, so look out for other signals that something is upsetting them. Dogs can also, rather cutely, catch a yawn from their humans and are more likely to do so from a person they are close to. Some dogs have a paw-ticularly dramatic yawning-style, a joy to behold. *See also* ANXIETY, WHALE EYE

YELPS

A plaintive yelp is a distress call, whether from pain or because they were startled by something, so be sure to pay attention to a yelp from your furry friend. *See also* COMMUNICATION, GROANS

YIP

A short, sharp and high-pitched bark, often excited. Puppies are particularly enthusiastic yippers. *See also* COMMUNICATION, YAPPER

YORKSHIRE TERRIER

A toy dog with big personality, the Yorkie's diminutive size does not match their self-importance. Their long silky hair can be cut into myriad hairstyles, and they have distinctive gold and steely blue colouring. Lots of socialization and training should keep the yaps at bay.

YOUTH

One minute you have a sweet pupper who's doing well with their training, and suddenly it has ap-paw-rently all gone out of the window when the doggy teens hit. It can strike at any time between six and twelve months and can last until they are two years old or longer, so be prepared for a ruff ride! Your fluffy teen is going through big hormonal and brain changes, and the impulse to get out and explore the exciting world around them is hard for them to control. They will try your patience, but it will pass and after this fur-raising chapter, a wiser and calmer dog should emerge. *See also* AGEING, PUPPIES

ZOOMIES

A bit like a toddler's sugar rush, these are common occurrences after food, or a walk, and ambush you most often in the evening. Common buffoonery includes charging around, attacking toys and humping, with the obligatory crazed look in their eye. If it isn't putting them at risk, or anyone else in the household, furry or otherwise, then sit back and enjoy the show. *See also* FRAP, INSANITY

ZZZ

Given their universal love of the snooze, how paw-some this dictionary should end catching up on a few well-earned doggy zzzs.
See also BEDS, BEDTIME, DREAMS, NAP, SLEEP

Sweet dreams, doggy

ACKNOWLEDGEMENTS

Following in the paw prints of *The Cat Lover's A to Z*, this book is also dedicated to my ever-supportive partner Ed, and cheerleading daughters, Edie and Rosa – thank you for putting up with me. I could not have achieved these books without them, and I will be fur-ever grateful for their input.

A big thank you to my wonderful agent Euan Thorneycroft and Jessica Lee at A.M. Heath, I really could not have found a more paw-fect team.

I am very grateful to Emma Foster for her vet's point of view and helpful suggestions, and Natalie Wood for her insight on dog behaviour and help with research ideas (any errors are entirely mine).

Thank you to my lovely and brilliant editor Sarah Thickett for commissioning this and *The Cat Lover's A to Z*. Sarah and all the team at Quadrille have been a dream to work with and I am so grateful for all their support. Particular thanks to Alicia House, Wendy Holden, Martina Georgieva, Emma Bastow and to everyone in the sales, marketing and comms team for all their hard work.

For further reading, I would recommend the information packed websites of the RSPCA (www.rspca.org.uk), Dog's Trust (www.dogstrust.org.uk), Battersea Dogs and Cats Home (www.battersea.org.uk) and Blue Cross (www.bluecross.org.uk). These excellent books have also been valuable resources in researching *The Dog Lover's A to Z*: *In Defense of Dogs* by John Bradshaw; *The Dog:*

A *Natural History* by Ádám Miklósi; *The Complete Book of Dogs* by Rosie Pilbeam; *Clever Dog* by Sarah Whitehead; and *Dog Training and Behaviour Solutions: The Stress-free Way to Live in Harmony with Your Dog* by the team from the Facebook group Dog Training Advice and Support (DTAS).

Thank you to all the Small Dots clients and customers for their support and to the following for their general paw-sitivity about the books: Nicola, Pete, Bella, Emily, Helen, Rich, Marlie, Lukas, Holly, Jim, Eva, Charlie, Nik, Jane, Jess, Jo, Gillian, Katie and all of the DD's, John, Cynthia, Martin, Marjorie, Finn, Max, Madelon, Valerian, Antonia, Joshua, Archie, Phoebe, Amanda, Steven, Amy, Clara and Eloise.

Finally some su-paw models must not be forgotten for their contributions – Chewie (see Best in Show), Archie (Baths), Kasper (Tongue Out Tuesday), Dorrit (Cockapoo), Laxey and Otis (Sticks), Flo and Womble (P), Juno and little Maisey (above).

Our heartfelt thanks to the following dogs for being such good girls and boys during the making of this book.

Labradors
Su-paw fans of: manky tennis balls
Fur-iends of: Harriet T

BREWSTER & DORA

KASPER

Miniature Schnauzer
Pre-furs to be: on guard
Fur-iend of: Clare

Jackapoo/Schnauzer
Also known as:
The Mozza
Fur-iend of: Harriet B

MINNIE

TACKALO

WILBUR

Parsons Russell Terrier
Full name: Tackalo Henry Gruffahound
Fur-iend of: Alice

Cockapoo
Last seen: stealing socks
Fur-iend of: Euan

· MAISEY ·

Cocker Spaniel
Mostly found:
burying bones
Fur-iend of: David

IZZY

Morkie (Yorkie/Maltese)
Mostly enjoys:
having a snooze
Fur-iend of: Natalie

DORIS

Border Terrier
Fur-avourite game:
tug-of-war
Fur-iend of: Stacey

· LOKI ·

LUNA

Norwegian Elkhound
Also known as: Lokaccino
Fur-iend of: Alicia

Golden Retriever
Fur-avourite pastime:
lying in puddles
Fur-iend of: Olivia

Clare Faulkner is the author and illustrator of *The Cat Lover's A to Z*. She is also the illustrator of the best-selling *The Little Book of Sloth Philosophy* and *The Little Book of Otter Philosophy*. Clare is a freelance graphic designer and has worked for a diverse range of clients, on book, brand and product design with her company, Small Dots. She lives in London with her family and a mischievous Siamese cat, who is not at all interested in this book.

MANAGING DIRECTOR Sarah Lavelle
COMMISSIONING EDITOR Sarah Thickett
COPY EDITOR Wendy Hobson
PROOFREADER Emma Bastow
DESIGN MANAGER Katherine Case
DESIGNER Alicia House
HEAD OF PRODUCTION Stephen Lang
PRODUCTION CONTROLLER Martina Georgieva

First published in 2024 by Quadrille Publishing Limited

Quadrille
52–54 Southwark Street
London SE1 1UN
quadrille.com

Cataloguing in Publication Data: a catalogue record for this book is available from the British Library.

ISBN 978 1 83783 207 1

Printed in China

MIX
Paper | Supporting
responsible forestry
FSC® C018179